APPRENTICESHIP CAREER PLANNING FOR TEENS

A COMPREHENSIVE GUIDE TO SECURING APPRENTICESHIPS IN HIGH-DEMAND INDUSTRIES WITHOUT TAKING ON YEARS OF COLLEGE LOAN DEBT

P.D. MASON

Copyright © 2023 - P.D. Mason - All Rights Reserved.

The content created within this book may not be reproduced, duplicated, or transmitted without direct written permission from the author or the publisher.

Under no circumstances will any blame or legal responsibility be held against the publisher or author for any damages, reparation, or monetary loss due to the information contained within this book, either directly or indirectly.

Legal Notice:

This book is copyright protected. It is only for personal use. You may not amend, distribute, sell, use, quote, or paraphrase any part of this publication without the express consent of the author and publisher equally.

Disclaimer Notice:

Please be advised that the information contained in this book is for educational and entertainment purposes only. All efforts have been executed to present accurate, up-to-date, reliable, and complete information. No warranties of any kind are declared or implied, Readers understand, acknowledge, and agree that the author is not engaged in the rendering of legal, financial, medical, or professional advice. The content within this book has been derived from various sources. Please consult a licensed professional before attempting any techniques outlined in this book.

By reading this document, the reader agrees that under no circumstance is the author responsible for any losses, direct or indirect, that are incurred as a result of the use of the information contained within this document, in, but not limited to, errors, omissions, or inaccuracies.

For my Dad.

Without your gentle nudge, I wouldn't have known my own potential.

I wouldn't wish any specific thing for any specific person - it's none of my business. But the idea that a four-year degree is the only path to worthwhile knowledge is insane. It's insane.

— MIKE ROWE

CONTENTS

Introduction ix

1. Apprenticeships Explained 1
2. Why Choose An Apprenticeship 27
3. Readying Yourself For Success 39
4. Supply And Demand 65
5. Gaining Skills, Not Debt 89
6. Apprentice Career Development 107
7. From Apprentice To Financial Freedom 117
8. It's A Bright Future 137
9. Successful Paths Through Apprenticeship 149
10. Final Thoughts 165

About the Author 176
Also by P.D. Mason 177
References 178

INTRODUCTION

Welcome to what unintentionally became my second Career Planning for Teens book. If you've read my first book: *Financially Smart Career Planning for Teens*, I sincerely thank you for the read and even more as you've now moved on to the second book. I feel it necessary to point out that this book is not written just for high school-aged young adults, as working adults looking for a career change may also benefit from it.

When I initially created the Career Planning For Teens book outline, I intended to publish it with nearly the same amount of apprenticeship-specific material as this book you are reading. Unfortunately, after the first draft of the Financially Smart Career Planning For Teens book, I realized that it wouldn't work as no one would want to read upwards of 70 to 75,000 words about Financially Smart Career Planning for Teens - so I had to make a decision.

The decision I needed to make was whether or not to go against my thought process and rewrite the first book altogether, as it was way too long and would require the omission of quite a bit of information necessary for this topic. The alternate option was to have two separate books packed full of information that might appeal to multiple groups of career seekers. In countries where college costs are high, alternatives to traditional college aren't discussed very openly. The decision to create separate books allowed me to expand this book's details to include the plethora of apprenticeship opportunities available in the US, UK, and Canada.

This book will shed light on the often difficult decision young adults face in high and secondary school. Many of you may or may not have had a career development curriculum in your schools, just as you may or may have yet to be told the whole truth about what opportunities are available for an affordable post-secondary education after graduation.

I'll speculate that if you did have some career planning classes, the message within those career planning classes likely was that every one of you and your peers has to attend college to become successful and have a happy and prosperous life. That is blatantly false and is what I call the "college is the only way" mentality. Some school districts in certain parts of the country are generalizing the topic of your career planning as it's assumed every student is thinking about college. Because of this lack of transparency within the career planning curriculum, colleges continue to flourish financially, and the student loan industry has become a behemoth of a for-profit business.

The most interesting part about the "college is the only way" conversation that I hope you will come to understand in this book; is that college is not the only way to a long and happy career of your choosing. College degrees are unnecessary for carving out a financially stable career that can provide you with years of healthy income.

Here's an interesting bit of information regarding college and the vast importance many high schools and secondary schools put on the conversations about college entrance exams, which, in the US, you're likely well aware are the SATs and the ACTs.

The United States' largest employer, the US Federal Government, administers over one million Armed Services Vocational Aptitude Battery (ASVAB) tests yearly to prospective military enlistees. The ASVAB is a follow-up to the Armed Forces Qualification Test (AFQT), the initial test for those wishing to join the military. The US Federal Government uses the placement scores of the ASVAB to determine job category classification for enlisted service members. In some situations, military service personnel can pick their job within the ranks of the US Military based on their ASVAB score. *Why is this relevant, you ask?* It is highly relevant to this book because, as the largest employer in the United States, the US Government uses a simple ***vocational aptitude test*** to determine the best placement for a person's military job. No SAT or ACT scores are required to enter the military. No general classes or prerequisites are required to join the military – just a handful of multi-subject tests measured as vocational aptitude markers that have nothing to do with any of the vast arrays of collegiate-level 101 classes that are highly expensive, and are also what we've been led to believe are the proverbial golden ticket to a long and happy debt-free life.

Research.com states that at the end of the 2018-2019 school year, 86% of the 3.2 million United States high school seniors that made up the graduating class of 2019 entered the state or private college system. Let me reiterate that 8.6 out of every ten high school graduates chose, applied, received an early decision or general acceptance letter, and then went to college. Only 14% (or 448,000) of those 3.2 million high school graduates stayed back that year and chose to defer their college plans or skip college altogether.

The stark comparison of that 86% number of 2019 college entrants is that between 2019 and 2020, nearly 24% of those full-time freshman undergraduate students dropped out of the same college they had started less than a year before.

Let's put those numbers into more understandable terms. In April or May of 2019, 3.2 million American high school students graduated high school, and 2.75 million graduates went to college in Fall 2019. By the end of the 2019-

2020 freshman year, for those 2.75 million students – a staggering 24% of that first-year class had left college within that school year, which translates to a group of 660,000 students having left college within their first year. So plausibly, hundreds of thousands of students within that group will now be affected by student loan debt that they may be paying for years.

What if the 24% of students that dropped out could have had less expensive alternative career path information spelled out for them in their high school career planning curriculum? What if the 24% of first-year college dropouts had known they could have found an apprenticeship that would provide them with a low to no-cost education that would yield them a successful lifelong career in any one of multiple high-demand industries begging for apprentices as there is a rapidly expanding labor shortage?

Would it have made a difference?

Maybe yes, maybe no. It's hard to say.

What's not hard to say is that the students who decided their college path was not the right decision for them now need to rethink their career plans. In addition, many former students undoubtedly have a school year's worth of student loan debt behind their names.

This book aims to educate and enlighten young adults about often stigmatized but very respectable career paths that start with an apprenticeship and provide years of in-demand career opportunities, benefits, an excellent pay structure, and more.

After reading this book, you will have additional insight into the career planning discussions that weren't discussed in your high school; and ideally should have been discussed within the guidance counseling departments. I will provide you with invaluable career planning information that can set you on the right track to having a lifelong career that starts with an apprenticeship and pays you during the workday to earn while you learn on the job. Nearly all apprenticeships provide a structured education program that results in graduation from that apprenticeship program with a degree, certificate, license, or credentials that confirm you have the skills and education to perform work in a skilled and technical occupational field.

I assure you that these careers and respective education paths can be had without the need for student loan debt which can impede anyone's ability to make valuable gains in their financial future as they start their career.

How can I make these assurances?

Years ago, I was a first-year college dropout statistic that found an apprenticeship that changed the trajectory of my life.

Several decades ago, I was a high school senior with no direction. My family lived in the central Midwest, my Dad was a blue-collar skilled tradesman, and my mother was a homemaker (that was the term back then for stay-at-home moms). We lived in an affluent suburb of a major metropolitan city, and I went to public school. The "college agenda," as I now like to call the curriculum taught at my public school, was blatant and oppressive. As students are still being told today, college was the only way anyone would make something of themselves. Going to college was the only way to ensure we would get a "good job," and being able to raise a family was what we were told back then as well.

As you're reading the introduction to this book, the details of why I dropped out of college don't matter, but I tell you about it in another chapter. It wasn't more than a month or two into my senior year of high school when I dropped out of that high school and set out on my own. I worked odd jobs for the next three years, hoping to make some gas money. I had moved around to a few different states, and the direction I was looking for as a high school dropout just seemed to never catch up with me.

After three years of trying to make a living from just a few resources, I returned to my hometown and stayed at my folks' house temporarily. That was when I realized maybe it was right what the high school teachers were saying - maybe college was the only way, and I had some decisions to make.

A few months after moving home, I decided I needed an education. So I got a few student loans and was accepted into a well-known state university about 100 miles from my hometown. I was pressured to pick a major even though I had no idea what I wanted my life to look like when I grew up, so I registered for several general ed classes and one college major-related class.

I went through the whole process of move-in day, furnishing a small studio-style dorm room that shared a restroom with the studio dorm room next to me, and I was ready to start my classes. Of course, I was prepared to be a college student by that time; I kept telling myself, as that's what they had told us, right? *College is the only way!*

Four years of a few classes a week and cold, windy walks across the campus to the furthest building possible from my dorm were ahead of me, and those were my first wake-up calls to my decision. Although college was filled with lots of activity and people, I still lacked the direction to figure out what I wanted to do.

I was doing what the public school teachers told us was the only way, but I didn't feel I had made the right decision. Even before I started my first class, I probably knew it wasn't the right place for me; it's hard to remember those details many decades later. However, I still remember that even as a college freshman in my early twenties, I was not ready for the college lifestyle or college experience. I certainly wasn't prepared for the college loan repayment plans that would soon be in my future.

I started that first year of college with good intentions, as that's about all I could emotionally tell myself to do. Nevertheless, I was optimistic, kept my head up, and "gave it the old college try." I remember sitting in one of my classes early on and looking around the lecture hall at how young every other student seemed. I was the oldest student in the room, I was sure of that, and it was depressing. That first week or so of classes was likely the beginning of the end of my first year in the traditional collegiate system, as it wasn't but a month later I dropped myself from every class I had registered for.

It would take me a few years to understand how student loan debt has a crippling impact on a person.

Fast forward a year or so after dropping out of that state university when someone convinced me that vocational school was the better way to go. I wasn't even sure I knew precisely what vocational school was at the time as I hadn't heard that term used in high school, but the person that suggested it assured me that it's easier to get student loans for a vocational school because "it's not really like a college," so I was interested if it meant I could finally have a career that all those adults kept preaching we needed.

Before the start of the next school year, I went through the enrollment process again, this time at the vocational school just down the road from the state university. Again I was required to decide what I wanted to do, so I picked a single-track program: auto mechanic technology.

In high school, I had a buddy whose folks had an oversized garage and an extensive set of tools, so the buddy and I were constantly tearing apart old cars attempting to get them running again or even running better than they were. I never considered in those high school years that I liked working on cars so much that it was what I wanted to do for a career. *I never gave it a single thought.*

My vocational school auto mechanics plan was short-lived, as it took only a few months to understand that my back wasn't cut out for leaning over a car engine for hours on end. I did get a few nice things from that experience though, I got to keep the middle-of-the-road starter set of auto mechanics tools the program required us to buy, and I also received a second round of student loan debt as a result of still not having a clearly defined path for myself and some insight into what I wanted my life and financial situation to be when I finally grew up.

The silver lining in those few years of "college is the only way" attempts is the higher education institutions where I attended were only an hour or so outside of my hometown.

So back home I went... again.

Once back home and after the dust had settled within me for a second try at becoming a college-educated and productive member of society, my father had witnessed enough of my trials and errors. So he sat me down one afternoon and discussed my "lack of prospects," as it could have been called.

He told me a story that I hadn't heard before, and that story he told wasn't all that much different than mine. As I came to understand it, my Dad had also just flailed around after his high school days. He also worked menial go-nowhere jobs as I had done, and somewhere in those years, he went off to the Navy, and after that, he married my mother, and they started a family. As a young family, my Dad was still searching for his career; but without a college education in the mid-1960s - it was a long road to success.

My father told me that he was given a stern talking to by one of his uncles, and that tough conversation was what he was about to have with me. My Dad then laid it out for me; I was to apply for the same apprenticeship my Dad's uncle told him to apply for. The rules, as my Dad explained to me, were the same rules he was given - apply for the apprenticeship, and if you don't make it, you'll apply again the following year. If you get accepted, you'll use the training and the earn-while-you-learn structure of the apprenticeship to start getting a foothold in your life and success. If, after you graduate from that apprenticeship and that line of work isn't what you want to do, you'll at least have a steady income and a skill to fall back on while you decide what you want to do.

I wouldn't realize it until many years later, but that stern talk was undeniably the best advice my Dad ever gave me.

I want to share with you one more quick story that was the defining moment of my choice to become an author and the very reason I had the idea for the topic of this book.

My oldest son was starting his career planning curriculum in high school. One day a notice came home from the school announcing that there would be a "college day" at the school, and parents were invited to attend with their children.

I read this information on the leaflet and then reread it. Finally, I read it a third time as I needed clarification that only our local state universities would be represented at college day, in addition to a few of our private colleges.

I was dismayed that no vocational school was listed as attending, nor was there any representation from any business or local jobs training programs.

The college fair happened, and I attended with my son... secretly unwillingly, but I did. I silently followed my son around and nodded my head quite frequently when he excitedly commented about this university or that college.

A few weeks after the college fair, I was at the school and ran into the Principal and asked for a minute of his time, to which he politely obliged. I asked, "How come the school only invited colleges and universities, and there weren't any vocational or trade apprenticeship programs there?".

The reply I received was so concerning to me that it still resonates.

The Principal explained that the school board would not allow them to participate.

I politely asked him to repeat himself as I wasn't sure I had heard him correctly, but unfortunately, I did. No representation of non-traditional higher education institutions would be allowed at the college fair, per the school board's direction.

Shortly after that interaction with the Principal, I decided I needed to do anything I could to get the word out about alternative career options that didn't require young adults to sign up for years of student loan debt. This was my first reason for feeling like I should tell my personal story, hoping it might help just one or two young adults develop a career plan that wouldn't financially burden them for years with college loan debt.

When that conversation happened with my son's high school principal, I had already known some young adults a year or two older than my son who had attempted college and dropped out. That surprised me, as I had known these kids, and they were intelligent, articulate, and seemingly driven young adults that, for whatever reason, didn't make it in a college environment.

I ran into one of those young adults during the high-school graduation season for my oldest son, and I asked that young man what had happened with his college plans.

The answer I received was, "College wasn't for me." I thought I was looking in the mirror and talking to myself during that conversation, as it was like I was whisked backward many years prior when trying to figure out my own life and career path.

I then asked that young man what his next plan was, and the answer came with a quiver in his voice. "Well, I guess I need to figure out how to repay the money I borrowed for that wasted year of my life." That young man is now thriving and living his best life as a trim carpenter for a local home builder, and he loves the work. He loves working with his hands and tools and the satisfaction of seeing his finished woodwork at the end of the workday.

This interaction with that young man was reason number two of why I felt I wasn't doing everything within my power to educate young adults about the options for an alternative career path.

Although a skilled or technical occupation may not be as glamorous as having four years of a well-known private college diploma or a three-letter Greek fraternity or sorority behind your name, careers that require technical training and often licenses, certifications, or credentials in a particular field are worthy of the stigma that still may be present for these careers. Most importantly, these lucrative careers can be had with very little out-of-pocket cost for the required education to succeed.

A handful of ideas stuck with me about how to get the word out about apprenticeships and their value from a career planning and financial standpoint.

When the ideas I had just seemed like they would target a small local audience in my area, it was then that I had the idea for a book, and this is why I thank you for reading this far.

I assure you every bit of material presented in this book comes from years of my own experience with multiple college attempts, run-of-the-mill jobs, struggling financially when my student loans kicked in, and the opportunity that changed my life - even though I didn't realize until years later just how that opportunity to become an apprentice would help define my career and provide me the financial freedom I had dreamt about as a young man.

Is being a skilled tradesperson who has worked in the construction industry for over 25 years a high-profile career? Definitely not. When I've had a rough day at work where my work boots and work pants are caked with mud, do I ever wish for a job where I don't have to wear a hard hat and have to work out in the rain? I most certainly do not.

Would I exchange one day in the career my Dad gently pushed me towards for a college degree and hefty student loans to work a nine-to-five office job? Not a chance.

In the following chapters of this book, I will tell you everything I know and have learned about apprenticeships in the quarter century since I first became an apprentice in a skilled trade working in the construction industry.

I am certainly not partial to any specific industry that offers apprenticeships, and I don't lean to one side or the other of the union vs. non-union discussion. If you don't know what that discussion is, settle in and keep reading because I explain it in Chapter 5.

In full transparency, I am a member of the United Association, just as my Dad was. The United Association is a National Union Trade Labor Organization that represents multiple skilled trades occupations such as plumbing and pipefitting throughout the US and Canada, but that has no bearing on this book or the purpose of the book. I want you to know that apprenticeships are available in many different industries, and many of those industries are represented by collective bargaining parent organizations, just as equally beneficial apprenticeships are available through private companies and private industry organizations.

The primary purpose of this book is to fill in the gaps in the career planning discussion that you haven't been told by parents, teachers, advisors, or anyone willing to be honest about the cost of college and the potential ramifications of acquiring student loans. For example, the information you haven't been notified of is that you can secure a lifelong career path that will provide excellent pay, benefits, and a financially sound retirement. This can be accomplished without needing a college degree and certainly without ever needing to secure college loan debt that will take years to pay off.

After reading this book, you will have more than enough information to continue researching on your own what in-demand industries and sectors are affected by a constantly shrinking workforce as the older generation is steadily retiring.

I'll provide you with details of those in-demand industries and what the typical apprenticeships are within those industries.

I'll tell you how long those apprenticeships last and what you can expect after you graduate from an apprenticeship. I'll also tell you the average costs for a four-year college path versus a low-cost apprenticeship education.

I'll detail the differences in apprenticeships between the United States, the United Kingdom, and Canada, as these three countries are the leading apprenticeship-driven countries of the world, and the labor shortage is not just consolidated in the United States.

Best (and probably most) of all, I'll tell you why starting your career in an apprenticeship that pays you every day to learn on the job; is the absolute most financially innovative way to start your working career.

By not having thousands or even tens of thousands of dollars or more of student loan debt to start repaying just six months after you receive a college diploma, you can decide where every penny goes that you earn as an apprentice and for the remainder of your career as a skilled worker. And, for what it's worth, skilled workers have just as much education to bring to their career as an Ivy League college graduate. You'll read in this book how many years I went to apprenticeship school, and this may shore up your understanding that apprenticeship programs have nearly the same hours required in a classroom setting as four-year colleges require for a degree.

Student loan debt is crippling for young adults that enroll in college, and the potential decades of repayment of those loans can be avoided when you choose an alternate (but not often talked about) career path in dire need of a new younger workforce.

I hope you enjoy this book, but more so than that - this book should provide you with enough information to do your research and make a well-informed decision about whether college is the right path for you or whether you'd be willing to take a chance on an apprenticeship that teaches you everything *(and I mean everything)* you need to know to pave your way towards an occupation in an in-demand industry where there's no shortage of work for career seekers like you.

I thank you again for supporting me by reading this book.

P.D. Mason

1

APPRENTICESHIPS EXPLAINED

What Is an Apprenticeship?

The word apprentice has many contextual meanings, but the definition states it's an arrangement in which someone learns a job, a trade, or an art from another person. Apprenticeships are most often described as on-the-job training, and the trainee is under the direction of and works under the direct supervision of the trainer.

Historically apprenticeships are certainly not a new idea, nor are they an invention that anyone can claim the right of discovery. Apprenticeship was first recognized centuries ago as an approved method to train the sometimes regarded as "untrainable" people. Those people would be closely monitored and educated in whichever field or task their Master deemed appropriate. Then, that

Master would house, clothe, and feed each "indentured" apprentice to the Master.

In the late 19th century and early 20th century, apprentices typically ranged in age from ten to seventeen years, and apprentices were not favored based on gender. Many sophisticated and well-to-do Lords and Ladies of the era would keep indentured apprentices on hand with the idea that each apprentice would learn a specific craft or skill. At the end of the contracted period, the noble family who provided for the indentured apprentice would then gain a faithful paid employee.

Fast forward a few hundred years, and the United States National Apprenticeship Act (NAA), sometimes called the Fitzgerald Act, was signed into law in 1937. This new law that regulated U.S. Government-sponsored apprenticeship programs allowed the US Department of Labor to control the welfare of apprentices regarding health and safety. Additionally, this 1937 law prevented discrimination against apprentices based on race, ethnicity, religion, age, and gender.

Throughout the initial years of this new NAA legislation, primarily skilled trades apprentices were provided with support. Eighty-six years later, apprenticeships are thriving in the United States. Many additional industries, such as healthcare, advanced manufacturing, and technology, have also adopted apprenticeship models to further their abilities to provide on-the-job training.

Most apprenticeships worldwide commence with the apprentice receiving agency-issued credentials in their field. The credential could be a completion certificate, a state-issued trade license to perform specialized work within a trade, or certifications for technical knowledge.

Did You Know?
George Washington was an apprentice surveyor before becoming President of the United States.
Before Elvis Presley was "The King of Rock' n Roll," he was an apprentice electrician.
Rock star Ozzy Osbourne was an apprentice plumber before he climbed on the Crazy Train.

THE MODERNIZATION OF APPRENTICESHIP

The documented history of apprenticeships and their structure dates back almost 4000 years ago in the Babylonian Code of Hammurabi, which said, "Artisans teach their craft to the youth." This was the earliest noted reference in history related to the skilled teaching of the unskilled.

America, the UK, and Canada were built through many centuries of apprenticeships and skilled labor. During the continuous period when the colonization of America by the English around the late 1600s, the English brought their key journeyman to the Americas to aid in building what was called "a new society."

Specialized craft workers were sent from England by the thousands, and many of those Master craft workers brought their domestic apprentices with them. Remember, during this period, the apprentice relied on his "Master" for the essentials, including food and shelter. This influx of skilled "craft" workers and their apprentices to America continued until the shift toward the Industrial Revolution in the late 1800s was imminent.

As the Industrial Revolution brought on rapid technological advances, those changes sparked new changes to the apprenticeship model and systems as we know them today. The Industrial Revolution focused on the era's technology, and machines were that new technology.

In the early 1920s, groups of construction industry professionals banded together to create reform within the apprenticeship system in America as it was still falling short. They hoped to form an organization that could craft a national apprentice system that would favor the apprentices and provide more rights, better working conditions, better pay, and skills above and beyond what was needed to earn their income.

As previously said, it wasn't until 1937 that the American Government would act and pass the Fitzgerald Act, which provided a registered apprentice program and added many safety measures and protections for workers' rights, including apprentices. Fast forward to the modern day, where the United States, Canada, and United Kingdom apprenticeship systems and programs run smoothly and afford many different opportunities for men and women throughout numerous industries.

According to the US Department of Labor Office of Apprenticeship, in 2022, there were close to 600,000 apprentices registered in nearly 27,300 Government approved apprenticeship programs throughout the US.

The passage of time has modernized the apprenticeship models to be fair, inclusive, and an avenue for which anyone wanting to enter the workforce or change careers can join an apprenticeship program. The modern apprenticeship models don't quite resemble those of the Lords and Ladies from centuries ago, and today's apprenticeships are focused on skills building, education, and sustainability for in-demand jobs across many industries.

An apprenticeship provides an "earn while you learn" structure, and you'll read that term quite often in this book as it is arguably the main reason why an apprenticeship is so attractive for secondary and high school students, in addition to adults looking for a career shift. This means you will work during the business day under a trained worker guiding you and teaching you how to do the tasks that a qualified or credentialed skilled worker has already learned. An apprentice will typically work a 40-hour week depending on the industry in which the apprentice works, and the apprentice will need a certain amount of documented classroom training hours, typically between 1500 and 2000 hours, over the life of the apprenticeship.

THE STRUCTURE OF APPRENTICESHIPS

When considering seeking an apprenticeship, you may first consider the two most recognized options that most apprenticeships are affected by. The options relate to how things are structured, like hourly pay rates, benefits such as health care, retirement savings, and paid time off. There are many different factors between the two options, and you will have to familiarize yourself with them and understand how their differences may affect your lifestyle.

There is no right or wrong option between the two; it depends on which option would better fit you.

Some questions you might want to ask yourself before we get into the explanation of the options are:

• Would I rather have a weekly paycheck, or is being paid once or twice a month sufficient?

• How much am I willing to spend on my education?

• If I feel under-compensated for my work, could I ask for a raise?

• Would I like to contribute to my retirement fund?

• If your apprenticeship job required hand and power tools, would you rather have tools provided for you or buy the tools you like to use?

• If you've ever worked a job where you've had performance reviews, did you like it?

The two options, which nearly mirror each other in the US, UK, and Canada, are generally referred to as:

• Collective Bargaining

• Non-Collective Bargaining

In many industrial or technological industries that support the apprenticeship model of training their workforce, Collective Bargaining is most often referred to as Union, Trade Union, or Trade Labor Union, and Non-Collective Bargaining is most often referred to as Open Shop or Non-Union.

To simplify the definition of the two options, a better way to explain them might be like this:

Collective bargaining is when a group of employees, usually represented by a union, negotiate with their employer or employers on working conditions, wages, benefits, and other employment terms. Collective bargaining aims to reach an agreement or contract that benefits both parties.

Alternatively, non-collective bargaining employers do not have a formal agreement or contract with a union or group of employees. In this case, the employer negotiates employment terms, benefits, and conditions with individual employees. This means each employee deals independently with the employer rather than as a group.

The main difference between collective bargaining and non-collective bargaining employers is the bargaining power of the employees. In collective bargaining, employees can typically negotiate from a stronger position because they have the union's collective bargaining power and a large labor workforce behind them. In non-collective bargaining, employees may have less bargaining power because they negotiate as individuals and may have different leverage than a group.

Overall, collective bargaining is a process that allows employees to negotiate better employment terms and conditions, while non-collective bargaining involves negotiations between individual employees and their employers.

There are also several key differences between collective bargaining in the US and Canada versus the UK. The main differences include the legal framework, bargaining structure, and union density.

In the US, collective bargaining is regulated by federal and state laws, while in Canada, the federal Government and each province set the legal framework for collective bargaining. In the UK, collective bargaining is not governed by specific laws but rather by a combination of common law and labor codes, which vary across different industries and sectors.

In the US and Canada, collective bargaining typically occurs at the individual employer or trade group level, with unions negotiating separate contracts with each employer or group. In the UK, however, collective bargaining is often conducted at the industry or sector level, with unions dealing with employer associations or trade groups to establish industry-wide or sector-wide agreements.

Union density, or the percentage of unionized workers, is generally higher in Canada and the UK than in the US. This can give unions in these countries more bargaining power, as they represent a larger share of the workforce and can exert more pressure on employers.

Other factors that can influence collective bargaining in the three countries include the political climate, the strength of the labor movement, and the cultural attitudes toward unions and collective bargaining. While there are certainly differences between the US, Canada, and the UK regarding how collective bargaining is structured and regulated, all three countries have a long history of labor activism and worker organizing and have significantly contributed to developing the modern labor movement.

Similarly, non-collective bargaining can give employees more flexibility in negotiating their employment terms and conditions. Rather than being bound by the terms of a collective bargaining agreement negotiated on their behalf, individual employees have more control over their wages, benefits, and working conditions. This can allow employees to negotiate better terms based on their unique skills, experience, and preferences.

It's important to note that potential disadvantages, such as reduced bargaining power and weaker job protections for individual employees, can offset the benefits of non-collective bargaining employment. Additionally, in industries with high levels of inequality or where workers face significant power imbalances, non-collective bargaining may lead to exploitation or unfair treatment of employees. Ultimately, the differences between collective and non-collective bargaining depend on various factors, including the specific industry, the employer's size and structure, and individual workers' preferences.

Here are some of the potential benefits of completing an apprenticeship within a trade union:

• Negotiated pay structure: Unions often negotiate higher wages for their members, as well as more structured and fair pay scales that consider experience, education, and job responsibilities.

• Benefits packages: Unions may negotiate for more comprehensive benefits packages, including health insurance, dental and vision coverage, life insurance, and disability insurance.

• Retirement planning: Unions may negotiate for retirement benefits such as pensions, 401(k) plans, or other retirement savings plans to help workers plan for their future.

• Job safety: Unions can help ensure workers access safe working conditions, proper equipment, and training to prevent accidents and injuries.

• Reduced working hours: Unions may negotiate for shorter workweeks, overtime pay, and breaks throughout the day to help workers maintain a healthy work-life balance.

• Job conditions: Unions may negotiate for improved job conditions, such as access to training and professional development opportunities, fair promotion policies, and protections against discrimination or harassment.

It's also worth noting that the benefits of union membership vary depending on the industry, the employer, and the particular union in question. Additionally, union membership may have downsides, such as union dues or potential conflicts with management. However, working for a trade union can offer a range of potential benefits that can help workers secure better pay, benefits, and working conditions.

Here are some different potential benefits of completing an apprenticeship within a non-union option:

• Potentially higher individual pay: Without union dues, non-unionized workers may be able to negotiate higher individual pay than unionized workers in the same role.

• Flexibility in benefits: non-unionized employers may offer more flexibility in benefits, such as choosing between different health insurance plans or opting out of certain benefits in exchange for a higher salary.

• Greater autonomy: non-unionized workers may have greater autonomy and control over their working conditions as they negotiate their terms of employment directly with their employer rather than being bound by a collective bargaining agreement.

• Fewer conflicts: non-unionized workplaces may experience fewer conflicts between management and employees, as no organized union can advocate for specific demands or potentially engage in strikes or other collective action.

• More fluid job roles: Without a rigid collective bargaining agreement, non-unionized employers may have more flexibility in assigning job roles and responsibilities, allowing employees to gain experience across different areas of the organization.

• Easier promotions: non-unionized workers may have an easier time securing promotions or advancing in their careers, as there is less pressure to follow strict seniority-based rules that can sometimes be found in unionized workplaces.

It's important to note that the benefits of working for a non-unionized employer can vary depending on the industry, the employer, and the individual employee's preferences and circumstances. Additionally, non-unionized workers may access additional job security, benefits, or workplace protections than unionized workers. As a result, they may be more vulnerable to exploitation or unfair treatment by their employer. Ultimately, the choice between working for a unionized or non-unionized employer depends on various factors, including the specific industry, the size and structure of the employer, and the individual worker's priorities and preferences.

As I've explained some of the differences between these two options, I cannot stress enough that neither of the options is better or worse. The unionized and non-unionized workforce can choose which option they prefer, and I assure you it all comes down to your preference for a few differences between the two options.

I have made acquaintance with many people through the years who have made successful and lifelong careers from either of the options. Of course, there is no right or wrong option that you need to be informed of as you gather information about apprenticeships, but these options may come up as a decision you'll have to make.

My apprenticeship many years ago was through a collective bargaining structured program. I asked myself some of the same questions years ago that I suggested you ask yourself, and I realized through asking myself those same questions that I wanted a paycheck every week. Although I could budget and manage my finances without needing help as a young man, at the very least, I wanted to be paid for my work every week.

Additionally, I've never liked asking a supervisor or boss for pay increases, just as I never liked asking to borrow money from anyone. Hence, those two questions were my deciding factor in following my Father's recommendation to apply for an apprenticeship. I would suggest again that you read over those questions and make some of your own decisions.

Depending on the industry or field of work that interests you, you may not have to choose between the collective or non-collective options. For example, if you are interested in an apprenticeship where collective bargaining does not represent the labor workforce, your only choice will be when you'd want to start your apprenticeship.

Not all industries are identifiable as Union or Non-Union, there may be some industries that don't have collective bargaining options for their apprentices and skilled workforce, so your only choice again would be the non-collective bargaining option.

Before I move on to some well-known and lesser-known industries that support the apprenticeship model, I want you to remember that whichever of the two options between collective and non-collective bargaining interests you more, there is no wrong choice.

Again, it's all about how you would like to manage your day-to-day within your career. I've listed some of the differences between a collective bargaining union and the non-union option, where you may have to negotiate with your company or your supervisor yourself.

As mentioned, I've known many non-union skilled tradespeople who love their work. They appreciate forming a perfect working relationship with their supervisor or boss. Relationship building is essential to those workers as they feel it suits them better and can provide better insight to their company management about their skills. In addition, it works well when asking for additional pay or more vacation time based on merit alone.

INDEPENDENT AND COOPERATIVE APPRENTICESHIPS

Apprenticeships need to be supported by the companies that rely on the apprentice pool as the work within that industry increases or decreases. For example, you could go to work one day as an apprentice and be told, "We've got work for the next two years," just as you could be called into your supervisor's office and be told, "The project you are on is wrapping up, and there may be a couple of days break while we find another project for you." This is a rare conversation that an employer might have with an apprentice, but it does occasionally happen.

Conversations like this happen in any industry you'll work in as an apprentice, as sometimes, in a skilled labor occupation, situations come up that mean your workday might be shortened due to weather, or there might have been an issue that takes a day or two to resolve. But, I assure you that the work will be plentiful as an apprentice, and it's rare that an apprentice doesn't have work.

Within any in-demand industry or sector, there are two types of structured apprenticeships: Independent and Cooperative.

Independent Apprenticeships are typically organized and managed by specific employers or maybe a group of same-industry employers who always would like a fresh stream of credentialed workers available to replace the folks who will retire or have decided to move on to something else.

The employers in an independent apprenticeship are not typically connected to a specific educational program to provide the required hours of classroom training, nor are they governed by an agency or a government entity to develop a classroom curriculum that mirrors the job training apprentices receive.

Here is an example for you. A fictional tech company, AppsForYou, needs help securing employees to write code for the apps they make for cellular devices and tablets. AppsForYou decides they would like to start a code writing apprenticeship that will provide them with future full-time skilled code writers for years to come.

AppsForYou hires "apprentices" to shadow some of their existing code writers, and those code writers may or may not be teaching those apprentices how to write computer code.

You are trying to learn as much as you can from the people you are shadowing, and some of those people are engaged and willing to teach, while others might not be as engaging as they want to write code and not be bothered.

You remembered that when you were hired, AppsForYou told you that as an apprentice, you'd be going to the AFY School of Coding, but they didn't tell you when it would start or the length of the education program. So you've asked around the building, and you're not getting many answers.

AppsForYou seems like they don't have a dedicated classroom instruction plan in place, and it appears they are figuring things out as they go.

How would this make you feel?

Independent apprenticeships in some industries can be managed very well. Also, they can deliver exactly what they promise, but it would be entirely up to you to ask the right questions and understand what they offer.

Cooperative Apprenticeships are organized in cooperation between employers and educational institutions and are managed by a governing body of individuals. The individuals may be educators, representatives of an employer company, trade-affiliated representatives, or others.

The cooperative apprenticeship is nearly always structured with a set curriculum as the apprentice moves through the program and regularly checks for proficiency within the classroom and the related training on the job.

Most apprenticeships in the US, UK, and Canada are cooperative apprenticeships, and all are designed for students to apply what they earn in the classroom to their respective levels of training in the field.

It's safe to say that nearly all of the collective bargaining union employers in the US, UK, and Canada are of the cooperative type, as cooperative apprenticeships are focused with equal importance being shared between the classroom and on-the-job training.

Cooperative apprenticeships rely on classroom training to validate what skills you are taught on the job. Job training requires classroom training to provide the theory and educational curriculum so you can associate what you see during the workday with what you are learning in the classroom.

Let's revisit AppsForYou as a cooperative apprenticeship employer. AppsForYou has decided they would like to start an apprenticeship program as they know they will be losing some employees in the coming years to retirement. They'd like to be able to train the replacements for those retirees in-house.

AppsForYou provides an apprenticeship development plan to a fictional organization called TechApprentices that regulates and oversees technology industry apprenticeships. TechApprentices reviews the AppsForYou apprenticeship plan and verifies the program contains a timeline of apprenticeship, proves that the apprenticeship is available to men and women of all ages and nationalities, and AppsForYou has provided an outline for an educational curriculum that AppsForYou will teach.

AppsForYou gets their apprenticeship development plan approved by TechApprentices, and AppsForYou now has a registered apprenticeship program that meets the guidelines of the apprenticeship program requirements set forth as regulated and required by TechApprentices.

You apply for an AppsForYou apprenticeship that is listed on a local jobs website, and within that apprenticeship listing is the job description for an app coding technician. Experience requirements are listed as none, and it also states that on-the-job training will be provided through an earn-while-you-learn program, and AppsForYou will provide classroom instruction at the in-house AFY training center. The company will pay your cost for some classroom materials and software you'll need, and the duration of the apprenticeship is eighteen months.

You get notified that you've been accepted into the AppsForYou apprenticeship and are requested to report to their building on a specific date at a particular time.

Seems pretty straightforward and exciting, doesn't it?

Apprenticeships are supposed to be fun, exciting, and challenging. They are supposed to be invested in your advancement, and they are supposed to be a path to your future career and a means by which to secure your financial future.

Independent and Cooperative apprenticeships are in place to give everyone a chance at a skilled career that will last a lifetime. Apprenticeships provide the avenue toward a structured education that will not leave you bogged down with student loan debt that may take decades to pay off.

APPRENTICESHIP REQUIREMENTS

The typical requirements to join an apprenticeship program vary between the US, the UK, and Canada. For example, the minimum age for entrance into an apprenticeship in the United States is 18 years old, whereas, in the United Kingdom, the minimum age is 16. In Canada, the rules are a bit different. Canada has minimal restrictions on minimum age requirements, which means children as young as 16 and adults are welcome to seek apprenticeships.

Canada has created an additional regulation for setting up their apprentice programs. The Canadian Government has designated thirty-nine skilled trades as Red Seal trades. Red Seal trades are job-specific trades with a common set of standards that apprentices must abide by and show proficiency through practical applications and the passage of exams. The Canadian Red Seal trades are very similar to various US licensed trades, as the licensed trades in America also require verified proficiency through on-the-job training and credentials through state or national agencies.

Some examples of Canadian Red Seal Trades that are similar to some of the US licensed trades are:

- Boilermaker
- Crane Operator
- Gasfitter

- Heavy Equipment Operator
- Electrician
- Ironworker
- Machinist
- Pipefitter
- Plumber
- Refrigeration and Air Conditioning Mechanic
- Sheet Metal Worker
- Fire Sprinkler Fitter
- Steamfitter
- Welder

Not every skilled trade in Canada is a Red Seal trade, just as not every skilled trade in the US or UK require credentials to work in that trade. Each country has different regulatory requirements for each licensed, credentialed, or competent person designation - and when you are in an apprenticeship, the goal is to complete that apprenticeship with the required credentials to work autonomously in those trade occupations.

APPRENTICESHIP TERMS AND DEFINITIONS

There are some standard terms and definitions used when explaining apprenticeships and how they work, many of which I've used in this book. Below are some universal standard terms used in the US, UK, and Canada. There are also some geographic-specific terms; those terms are shown with the specific country in parenthesis as (US) (UK) (CA).

Advanced Apprenticeship (UK): A level 3 qualification with equivalency education criteria as an A level.

Apprentice: A person who agrees upon employment to learn a specific trade or profession and is registered with the regulating authority. An apprentice may also have a private company sponsor.

Apprenticeship Committee: An oversight committee generally responsible for an apprenticeship program's training and education curriculum. Apprenticeship committees may also act as fiduciaries if public or membership contributions fund an apprenticeship program.

Apprenticeship Levy (UK): An apprenticeship levy is a taxation forwarded to UK employers to fund new apprenticeships.

Apprenticeship Standards (UK): a United Kingdom Government approved document stating the known definitions, job roles, lengths of apprenticeship, competencies, and entry requirements of an apprenticeship occupation.

Assessment Criteria (CA): An apprentice must achieve a performance standard for a specified learning element.

Autonomously: The freedom to work independently or alone.

Basic Skills (CA) (UK): The minimum level of essential technical skill needed to work within a trade and become an apprentice. Basic skills are proficiency within the trade.

Canadian Council of Directors of Apprenticeship (CCDA): The Canadian Government officials responsible for managing and directing the apprenticeship programs.

Challenge Exam (CA): The method of assessment for students to take just an exam for an apprenticeship course to prove their knowledge.

Collective Bargaining: the negotiation of workforce wages and other conditions of employment by an organized and collective group of employees. They are typically referenced as "Unions" or "Trade Unions."

Credential: a certification, certificate, trade license from a state agency, or a diploma stating successful completion of an apprenticeship program.

DAS (UK): Division of Apprenticeship Standards. The DAS promotes, services, and develops apprenticeship programs in the Commonwealth.

Employer: A business or organization that employs registered apprentices. The employer must provide on-the-job training for all apprentices in its employ.

Fringe Benefit. A benefit paid by an employer to employees or organizations that represent employees (such as a collective bargaining union) that may contribute to health care, retirement funds, paid time off, or additional categories. Fringe benefits are typically pre-tax monetary benefits for the employee.

JJAC: Joint Journey worker and Apprenticeship Committee: See Apprenticeship Committee. It also can be referenced as JJATC, Joint Journeyworker Apprenticeship Training Committee.

Journeyworker (Journeyman, Journeywoman): A credentialed skilled tradesperson who has demonstrated the skills, knowledge, and experience in which to practice their trade.

Merit Pay: A Merit pay structure is also called a pay-for-performance structure. The method typically allows for salary increases based on criteria set by the employer. This pay structure requires employment reviews and possible negotiations for future pay increases.

Non-Union (open shop): Non-union refers to companies that, although they might employ skilled workers, do not participate in collective bargaining agreements with local labor unions.

OJT: On-the-job training. The employer usually provides them. A skilled trainer will educate and guide apprentices on the field skills needed based on the specific trade. OJT is required in nearly all US, UK, and Canadian apprenticeship programs.

Prevailing Wage: A specific range of wage rates determined by the Department of Labor Standards that govern all worker's rates of pay on construction projects funded by public contributions.

Sponsor: An individual, company, organization, or committee who will sponsor the apprenticeship of one or more individuals. Sponsors may be regarded as the employer in situations where the apprentice has worked for the employer before acceptance into an apprenticeship program.

Stepped Pay: A stepped pay system incorporates a clearly defined method of employee wages. Stepped pay increases typically follow a defined timeline of pay increases.

Term of apprenticeship: The selected model is used as the baseline and milestones in determining apprentice eligibility to complete their apprenticeship. In the US, UK, and Canada, nearly all of the apprenticeships will be administered under one of these models:

HOURS-BASED MODEL. A required number of hours to be worked under the supervision of a credentialed journey worker.

CREDENTIAL-BASED MODEL. A competency certificate, credential, certification, or trade license must be obtained as proof of knowledge and experience in the individual trade.

COMBINATION/HYBRID MODEL. A combination of hours-based and credential-based terms of apprenticeship. Competency must be displayed through hours, evaluation, and credentials.

As we close out this chapter, I will remind you that apprenticeship programs can be found throughout the United States, the United Kingdom, and Canada, and not all apprenticeship programs are modeled after each other. Many apprenticeship programs have distinct differences, just as some will have similarities and minor differences between union and non-union apprenticeships. Although there are a few differentiating types or structures of an apprenticeship, an apprenticeship route to a solid career path is well worth the time investment in which to complete your on-the-job training and any required classroom work.

2

WHY CHOOSE AN APPRENTICESHIP

The best answer to the question of why someone should seek an apprenticeship is: *it is a great way to start a successful and sustainable career!*

We've previously discussed that apprenticeships are very budget-friendly, and often a person can manage the education tuition costs from their weekly or bi-monthly paycheck.

High school students like you that might be looking for an alternative to the high cost of college, which sometimes comes with years of college tuition debt, can set themselves up to be financially ahead of their peers by entering an apprenticeship.

Apprenticeships provide on-the-job training right from the beginning of a program. This job training also comes with a good starting pay structure right from the start. A typical apprentice pay structure is stepped or incremental pay as you gain experience and time in your apprenticeship. Your rate of pay and benefits will also increase regularly as you advance through the program and prove proficiency through your job performance or exams.

APPRENTICESHIP OR COLLEGE?

Although College or University has long been the curriculum taught in high and secondary schools, that doesn't mean it is the best option. Many high school or secondary school seniors are told they must "pick" a college before a particular month of their last year. If you were told "college is the only way," I assure you that you weren't given all the information to decide about college or career planning.

Although traditional college or university is the right choice for some, it may be the wrong choice for many of your peers, and quite possibly for you too – and that is entirely OK as that's why you're reading this book! I am very confident that by the time you've read this book's last words, you'll know what choice you'd like to make.

Traditional higher education institutions in the United States are state-funded or private institutions. Many of these institutions are for-profit, and their tuition reflects that they need substantial revenue to keep operating. The rising cost of post-secondary education has not stalled in recent years, making some high school students rethink their options of going the traditional four-year college route or finding an alternative.

The best alternative to entering a college or university's standard four-year program is to seek an apprenticeship. Within an apprenticeship, apprentices are learning new skills on the job, often daily. Imagine going to your earn-while-you-learn job every day, and by the time you go home, you've already learned two or three new skills. That's what an apprenticeship is all about - training. As you continue to learn new skills in your selected industry or field, you will feel pride when you can install a piece of equipment because someone had just taught you how to do it, and now they are letting you perform those tasks autonomously.

A SNAPSHOT OF COLLEGE COSTS

Have you thought about the true and accurate cost of college? Do you wonder whether you'll have to take loans for the tuition, food, and incidentals like books, toiletries, snacks, and the occasional night out?

Let's face it, if there were any way I could explain the financial difference between college and an apprenticeship to you more straightforwardly - I would. College is expensive, and although I won't say there's absolutely no benefit in choosing a college path, would you still prefer the college path if I told you that the money you save in student loans and the interest on those student loans could make you a millionaire in thirty years? I will show you just how this can happen in a later chapter.

Part of the ongoing problem that high school students face when choosing a college is that many adults and possibly your parents may still be stuck in the mindset that college is the only way.

A Gallup poll a few years ago stated that the percentage of parents wanting their children to attend college the year after post-secondary graduation was a staggering 54%. That number may not seem high (it's only about half, right?), but it's not the number that struck me as enjoyable when I first heard it - it was that *the parents wanted their children to head off to college.*

You may be in this position right now, where your parents are talking to you about college, as your high school graduation may be right around the corner, or it could be in a few years. Parents are natural planners, so they might be thinking about your options after high school just as much or maybe even more than you are.

The statement in that Gallup poll isn't surprising, as parents only want the very best for their children. Of course, you probably could agree that your parents only want the best for you as well, but if "the best" for you and your potential four years at college or university means you would be in some serious debt for the next twenty years or so, is that really "the best"?

I'm sure it's tough for you to comprehend the implications of a few decades of student loan debt that can negatively affect more areas than just your pocketbook.

What if you could paint the perfect picture in your mind of what your life would look like after college? Would you want to travel? Would you expect you could land your dream job for the highest salary you could've ever imagined? Would you like to settle down, get married and start a family?

All those daydreams are perfectly normal; I certainly had them in high school. What I didn't have, however, was a handle on some financial decisions that would negatively affect me for many years after I decided to leave high school and go out on my own.

VOCATIONAL SCHOOL TO APPRENTICESHIP

There is an additional but also lesser-known path into an apprenticeship that I talked about in the first book I wrote about alternative career planning titled: *Financially Smart Career Planning for Teens: The Roadmap To Making Informed Decisions In An Uncertain Job Market, Prevent Feeling Overwhelmed & Analysis Paralysis To Achieve Affordable College Degrees.*

The first book was more of a deep dive into the differences between the preparation needed for the application process and the selection process for college, in addition to comparing the cost of a college degree versus the lower price of a vocational degree. As vocational schools are more hands-on oriented and typically are two-year programs for a specialized occupation, the Applied Science degree or Associate of Applied Science degree one can achieve in Vocational School is commendable. Those degrees will offer you very well-paying opportunities to follow your career.

Some hands-on vocational school programs are two-year classroom programs that, once completing the program and receiving your diploma, may offer the opportunity to get into an apprenticeship through a private business type of apprenticeship which we will discuss in this book.

The Vocational School to Apprenticeship path is just as critical as everything I'll present in this book - it's a different way to achieve the same result. There is a caveat, however.

If a person wants to pursue that path, they can expect to pay around 10-20 thousand dollars a year for vocational school education, which may lead some people to student loan debt.

Vocational school graduates can then seek either apprenticeship, choosing between a union collective bargaining apprenticeship or a private company apprenticeship.

Graduates from a vocational school program are typically offered a spot in an apprenticeship or paid internship to gain their required field hours before taking exams to receive their credentials.

The vocational school to apprenticeship path is otherwise nearly identical to everything explained in this book.

Suppose you are a student that would like to explore the vocational school path. In that case, it's possible that after leaving a vocational school with a typical two-year degree in a hands-on technical industry, you could bypass several years in a multi-year apprenticeship. The benefit of paying the 10-20 thousand dollars a year for your two-year vocational school program would mean that you would become a credentialed worker sooner, which means you would be at full pay for a hands-on skilled worker in that occupation.

I have known multiple people who have started their careers in a vocational school program, received their required classroom instruction hours for their selected field of work, and then secured apprenticeships that they made very nice careers out of. These individuals have told me they appreciated the opportunity to step up or "fast track" their career by getting most of the schooling out of the way and then doing their required fieldwork.

The only drawback to doing your schooling first and following up with your fieldwork is that you may miss some educational or technical points that you might understand better if you can visualize what you see on the job with current educational topics in a classroom.

The vocational school to apprenticeship path is an option at the start of your career. If someone were to ask me which is better, between a paid on-the-job learning apprenticeship or a vocational school to apprenticeship path, I would tell them either one will get the same result.

The cost of vocational school may be a hindrance for some people, so people considering a vocational school as a path to an apprenticeship might be better suited with the on-the-job training model combined with in-classroom training, which are the typical apprenticeships we've been talking about.

EXPENSIVE MISTAKES

Earlier in this book, I told you about my college and vocational school attempts and how I thought I was on the right path, as that was still what people were telling me to do with my life because it "was the only way to a career." But unfortunately, those two failed college attempts were very costly, and I paid a financial and emotional price for many years to come.

I was twenty-one when I decided to attend a state college and sign the paperwork to fund my college entirely with student loans. As I told you in the introduction of this book, my attempted first year of college was short-lived as, within about three months, I was no longer going to classes.

I can't remember exactly how much my student loans were at the time, but given it was a state university I was attending - the cost of tuition, housing, and a meal plan back then was around $18,000 per year. Since I had only attended for a portion of my first semester, we can assume my student loan was $9,000 as I wouldn't have taken a second disbursement of the student loan money.

When I decided to attend vocational school the following year (remember I thought I wanted to be an auto mechanic because my buddy and I liked to "tinker" around on cars?) I also secured a student loan. As this was a vocational school, the tuition wouldn't have been as much as the university, so let's assume the school tuition was only around 30% of the state university tuition, making it $5,400. By the time I went to the vocational school, I was living in an apartment and had a roommate, so I didn't need to take the full tuition, which included housing, so at least that was helpful.

So, the $9,000 loan from the state university and the $5,400 loan from the vocational school from a few decades ago gave me a debt of $14,400 as a young man of around 22 or 23 years old. I don't recall what the interest rates were on those loans, and I also don't remember what the projected monthly repayment would have been, but it doesn't matter.

What matters in this re-telling of a few years of bad decision-making is that I should never have attempted either of those "college tries," as I could barely support myself, much less repay the lenders of my student loans. I was running from those loans for the next few years and didn't know how to fix it.

At some point over the next three to four years, I became familiar with a term called "garnishment." Garnishment is a bad word, and I wouldn't recommend that you get too familiar with it as I wouldn't wish that term on anyone. Garnishment is the term used when someone (or some entity like a business or a government) can take money out of your paycheck to repay a debt, and that's precisely what happened to me after a few years of running from those small student loans. I don't want to imply I wasn't attempting to pay those loans because I was - it was just that the small payments I was making to those loans did not seem to be reducing the loan amount as the interest on the loans was gaining quicker than I could pay the loans down.

The loans did end up with a zero balance after several years, and that was a huge life lesson for me that I hope you will never have to endure. I used that life lesson as my roadmap to define what I wanted my financial future to look like after I had all that loan repayment settled, and I have diligently stuck to that roadmap ever since. During that time, when I had loan creditors calling me threatening to do this and that, I promised myself I would never put myself in that position again, and I haven't strayed from that promise.

I will continue telling you more about student loans and some of the numbers behind the methods in a later chapter, so I want to close this chapter by telling you that if you feel a college path is your best option, that's great! Go after it, and I wish you all the best! If you want a bit of an advantage over your peers in the next three to five years, then keep reading!

Apprenticeships are conceivably the new "college degree" as apprenticeship has so much upside. However, few people talk about apprenticeships because it's not a well-known and accepted alternative to college. In addition, secondary and high schools aren't providing enough information about apprenticeships in their curriculum, and that's also part of the problem. High schools still think "college is the only way," and they're wrong.

As you continue reading the following chapters, I hope you are gradually enlightened to how choosing an apprenticeship far outweighs the time commitment and the monetary investment into a traditional four-year college plan as a means to start your career. It is also appropriate to remind you that I am not anti-college; I am overly passionate about educating young adults about the benefit of an apprenticeship and how to start your adult working career debt-free.

Interestingly enough, my middle child shut me down when he was in high school when I wanted to have the apprenticeship vs. college discussion with him. His mind was already made up even before I approached him about which private college he wanted to attend and what his major might be.

It wasn't but two years after he started college that I found myself driving to his college to clean out his dorm room as he realized that a collegiate plan wasn't his path, and he left college with student loan debt that he is repaying and is taking a bite out of his monthly income.

3

READYING YOURSELF FOR SUCCESS

INTERESTS AND SKILLS OF AN APPRENTICE

This may be the first time you've ever learned about apprenticeship, or even possibly you've never heard the term apprentice before, and that is certainly fine! What I am trying to provide for you is the most information I possibly can, related to most of the typical topics I've given talks about for many years.

I've spent hours talking to existing apprentices, brand new apprentices, and graduates of apprenticeship programs to get their feedback and insight on what makes a good apprentice candidate and what that person's feelings are on how apprenticeships could be better.

In this chapter, I will explain things that I know make a good apprentice and share some of the feedback I've received from others over the years. I'll also provide some expert feedback (expert meaning the available data from the organizations and agencies that manage and facilitate apprenticeships), so let's jump right in.

If we try to understand the typical apprentice's interests, it would be a very long conversation with possibly hundreds of bullet points or more, so I don't want to provide you with all of that data.

Every apprentice in every trade or occupation has entirely different interests than the next person, and there is no correct answer for what interests an apprentice should or could have.

Imagine you're approaching your high school or secondary school graduation and heard about apprenticeship as an excellent way to a financially stable career with the bonus of not having excessive student loan debt. Still, you're having trouble narrowing down the possibilities of what you'd like to do for your career.

Imagine that while researching apprenticeships, you get tired of browsing the internet and switch back to the video games you love playing. As you start the game, you realize that much of your downtime is spent playing video games, and the lightbulb above your head comes on!

You love playing video games, and you've told yourself many times that you could probably design a better game than the one you usually play - so, guess what?

You've just defined an interest!

It doesn't take too much time to define your interests for yourself. When I give talks to groups of apprenticeship information seekers, I ask them:

• What do you consistently like to do in your spare time?

Consistently is emphasized as shooting the basketball daily, day after day, whereas doing different activities a time or two a week is considered more occasional than consistent.

• Do you consider yourself a people person or more of a lone ranger type?

This can be a tough one, as I fully understand that you may have times when you like to be social, and there will be times when you want some downtime to scroll through social media. The idea behind this question is would you like to work closely with a team of people, or do you prefer to do everything yourself from start to finish?

There is no wrong answer to that question! Everyone (including myself) can likely give a vague answer, and yours may be too.

Here's another question for you:

• How committed are you to finding a successful career and creating financial freedom?

Again, this question might be subjective, but you must ask yourself.

I have found that the people that go all in on their apprenticeship turn out to be the most successful in their career choice, and if you can commit to the timeframe of an apprenticeship, you will sail right through to starting your career!

I keep touching back on the financial freedom topic, and I think I'd better clarify a few things for you so you understand fully where I'm coming from.

College is expensive; we've established that. However, not all colleges are affordable, and I know with certainty there are four-year college programs totaling around 100K in tuition, room, and board for the entirety of the four years. So twenty-five thousand a year for four years isn't all that bad, right?

If you received very little grant money to cover some of the 25K a year, it would help - but it likely would be a small portion, 10-15%. So let's say for the sake of the story that your total out-of-pocket costs for that four-year degree at a well-regarded middle-of-the-road college will leave you with 85 thousand in student loan debt.

Six months or so after you've graduated college or university, you'll have to start paying back those loans, but... what if you haven't received any job offers and cannot start paying at that six-month mark?

We will dive deeper into college loans in a later chapter, and I'll tell you about the what if's that may enhance your decision to seek an apprenticeship.

So, I've explained to you the three questions I like to ask new apprentices that I meet, and I hope you can do some reflection and come up with your answers, or at least maybe a few items that you'd consider your solutions. The questions are just a "toe in the water" to determine whether an apprenticeship is right for you.

A website in the UK called *NotGoingToUni* was very well done, and if you visit the website, you will find some great blogs and insights into the world of apprenticeship. They also detail some case studies of apprentices they have followed through their apprenticeship training.

Even though the website *NotGoingToUni* (notgoingtoiuni.co.uk) is based and written in the UK, the terms, ideas, and basis of why apprenticeships are so important are shared between the US, UK, and Canada. Please visit the websites mentioned in this book to research your apprenticeship further.

NotGoingToUni comments that the 6 Skills and Traits for apprentices should include the following:

- Passion
- Determination
- Resilience
- Communication
- Willingness to Learn
- Ability to Work Autonomously

I'm not going to relay the paragraphs of explanation that Not Going To Uni has provided for each of these six Skills and Traits, as I think it's a bit wordy. So instead, I will give you my perception of each of those from a former apprentice's standpoint, what I've learned about the skills and traits, and what I feel you can do as an individual to qualify or validate that you have some of these skills and qualities.

I wouldn't expect you to relate to everything I mention for the six skills and traits, but I hope you can take my explanations and try to associate them with something similar in your life that would indicate, yes, I'm ready to be an apprentice!

Passion. I will be brutally honest with you and say that I don't think there's been one day in my more than a quarter-century career as a construction tradesperson where I've thought I was overly passionate about my apprenticeship and career choice.

My apprenticeship was long, five years to be exact. At times, keeping my head in the game was mentally challenging, primarily due to the birth of two of my children while I was in the apprenticeship. I was working my apprenticeship job during the day and was taking my apprentice classes twice weekly in the evenings during the school year. It was mentally taxing on me to know that my wife was home managing, at first, one child, and then two years later, managing two toddlers while I was in classes. I didn't feel like a supportive spouse for two nights a week, but I committed to completing my apprenticeship, and my wife was fully supportive, and I worked through those feelings.

If you join an apprenticeship to start your career, you might be in a similar situation. You might have commitments or things happening outside of apprenticeship training that you'd rather be doing instead of taking classes. Still, you committed to an apprenticeship, which requires classroom education. *What do you do?*

Although it may sometimes not be where you want to be, showing up for your classes shows dedication, even if it's just a tiny amount. Understanding what you need to fulfill your obligations proves that you are invested in your career, and *that is passion.*

Determination. Think of your favorite sports figure. Do you think that person wants to be on the field every single game they show up for? I'm guessing they don't because maybe they are missing their child's birthday party, or perhaps their parent is sick, and they'd rather be comforting that parent.

That sports figure is determined to put their best face on, mentally block out distractions, and go out on the field where many people are there to see that sports figure in action.

Everyone has good days and some not-so-good days. It's hard as a high school or secondary school student to think that once you walk across that stage and accept your diploma, that well..... that's it... that's the end of your student life, and now parts of the real adulting world will start creeping in on you.

When you choose an apprenticeship, you must commit to seeing it through to the end, as you won't fully realize the benefit until your finish. Of course, when you complete your apprenticeship, you will be at the excellent full pay scale with full benefits; that is the fully realized benefit of an earn-while-you-learn training program that provides every bit of training and schooling you need to have a sustainable and lifelong career. But I promise you that if you get out of the apprenticeship and realize it isn't the career path you wanted, *you can walk away with your head held high!*

Remember earlier in this book when I explained that my Father gave me an "out" when he sternly suggested I seek an apprenticeship? The out he was talking about was just what I described above; you can walk away from an apprenticeship at any time without consequences. That's why the skill of determination is so important to have.

If you are determined to enter an apprenticeship, you should be just as determined to complete that apprenticeship and be further determined to have a long career in that industry!

Resilience. In the apprenticeship world and especially in the earn-while-you-learn model of apprenticeships, you will find some days harder than others.

You may be learning new skills you don't completely understand yet. You may have journey workers or trainers explaining things so fast that you don't have time to take mental notes.

You also may reach a point where your confidence starts breaking down as the concepts and methods you are supposed to learn aren't making sense.

I assure you that every apprentice I've ever had where I was their trainer and nearly every apprentice I talk to has had days like this.

Let's say for a moment that I take you on as my apprentice in my widget factory. The widgets we make in our factory are the most technologically advanced widgets to date, and many companies worldwide are using these widgets.

As I am transferring to another department, I must train somebody to do my supervisor job at the widget factory to keep up with production. I've already let you know that the training program is for three months, and after that, you'll be on your own as I've taught you everything you'll need to know.

While we're in the three months of training, I give you many hands-on tasks you can learn and many process-related explanations of why we make the widgets the way we do.

On the day I hand over my keys to the widget factory to you, I give you a short skills test to validate that I've done the right job of training you. But, unfortunately, you take the skills test and don't get satisfactory marks to prove you are ready.

I'd assume you would be pretty upset, but the fact that you didn't pass the skills test doesn't solely rely on you - as at least two people are involved in an on-the-job training apprenticeship. One person is the eager learner, and one person is the trainer. If both people don't give it their all, someone will be shortchanged.

You go home that day after work knowing that you failed the skills test and are pretty frustrated and may even be thinking about not returning to work the next day, even though I was very accommodating to the situation and understood it wasn't entirely your fault that you didn't pass the test.

You think about the situation that night at home and know what to do. You wake up early the following day, and you're the first one to the widget factory, and you are waiting for me to unlock the doors for you.

You are back at it and ready to go. Maybe even with a new level of excitement.

That is what's called being resilient. You don't let a slight hiccup ruin your day, much less your chance of getting those keys. Instead, you bounced back from a problematic situation and went right back at it.

Within apprenticeships, there are many widget factory days where things turn out wrong. They may be frustrating and aggravating, but if you have the resiliency, you can shake it off and return to work. That is a great skill.

Communication. Let's revisit the widget factory and use the same example about obtaining the keys to the factory and the skills testing. The scenario is the same, except one crucial factor didn't happen as the timeline was laid out. Can you think of what that factor is?

Communication?

That's exactly right! Communication seemed to be lacking at the widget factory. So even though you were listening and processing as much of the information as you could absorb daily, you likely weren't asking the right questions.

The fault in the situation lies evenly between you and the supervisor, so this is not to say you did anything wrong. However, this is your apprenticeship, and you're just trying to learn - and often, that can overshadow some fundamental principles.

At the widget factory, you are the apprentice, and your supervisor is your trainer. For you to learn, you need to be taught. For a trainer to teach, that trainer must remember that an apprentice is assumed to be coming into the apprenticeship with little to no knowledge of the industry and, quite frankly, likely the occupation.

If you're the apprentice trying to learn on the job, you must ask questions when you don't understand what a trainer is telling you. Alternatively, the trainer must ensure you know the material as the trainer presents it.

The one thing I've learned while training apprentices on the job or in my classroom is that when apprentices first start, they likely don't have the confidence to ask questions, possibly for fear of feeling unworthy as an apprentice. I assure you this is the opposite mentality an apprentice should have. You cannot learn unless you ask questions.

Additionally, a trainer should never under any circumstance, assume that an apprentice understands the explanation of a task by how the trainer explains it.

An old saying is that you will get five different answers if you ask five people to describe an orange. That also rings true in on-the-job training and apprenticeship; five people could explain the simplest tasks in five different ways.

No two people are alike, which means everyone has a difference in the way that they learn and the way that they train.

Just remember, asking questions is for the consumption of knowledge from someone else, and if you don't understand their knowledge as they've explained it, you should ask them to rephrase the answer or ask another person the question altogether.

Willingness To Learn. By reading this book you are already researching apprenticeships and how they can jump-start your career and financial future, which is an excellent sign that you are willing to learn!

People who already know about a specific topic or task don't usually sign up for an extended learning program, as they know or think they know enough to succeed.

When you have the willingness to learn, it means you are open-minded to a lot of new ideas, concepts, and even things you have no clue about - and just by you still reading this book with all of the material I've presented to you so far again convinces me that *you have the DESIRE to learn!*

I have seen many adults come through my apprentice classes, and I also teach continuing education classes for credentialed journey workers regularly. When I was chatting with another apprenticeship teacher from a different part of the Midwest a few years ago, we both talked about how much we enjoyed being instructors for adult learning programs.

The fellow I was talking to taught me a new word that describes folks like us, who are in the last portions of our careers, have crested the hill, and are now on the downhill slope planning for our retirements in a handful of years.

The word was "Andragogy" - pronounced (andra-gah-jee). The definition is easiest explained as understanding and putting into practice the science of teaching adult learners or the method and technique of teaching adult learners.

When we first started talking about the traits of an apprentice, I told you that I don't think I ever had a true passion for my trade and occupation. I should have clarified that by saying my "day job" occupation in the construction industry.

I have been blessed and lucky to have had over a quarter century of safe and steady work at my day job, starting with an apprenticeship. However, it wasn't until the last decade that I figured out what defined my "passion" in my work.

That passion is teaching and educating new apprentices that come through my classroom. I take it as seriously as I take my day job, and my day job is the primary income that pays the bills, so I hope as you've read this far and as you continue to read - you have a deep understanding of my passion for apprenticeships and just how life-changing they can be for people.

Apprenticeship leads to a lifetime career you might never have thought about, and an apprenticeship can mean the difference between having money in your pocket and in the bank or making continual student loan payments for years with outrageous interest rates, in which you may never get caught up.

Apprenticeships are genuinely life-changing, and I've seen it in men and women of all ages. The youngest apprentice I've had in one of my classes was 18, and the oldest apprentice I've had was 49 years old when he decided to make the change from a well-paying corporate job that he was burnt out on to an apprenticeship that started his wage about 40% less than he was earning in the corporate world. I asked this gentleman how he would manage the decrease in pay, and he said, "I needed a change because I was so unhappy doing what I was doing; I'm determined to make this work, and the temporary step backward in pay is well worth the reward in a few years."

That fellow has the qualities that fit right into an apprenticeship plan.

Ability To Work Autonomously. Let's first define autonomous. Autonomous is loosely defined as "having the ability to oversee oneself and manage one's affairs."

The word autonomous can easily be switched to "alone" based on the loose definition I told you. However, working autonomously in an apprenticeship is nearly as important as communication and the other four traits we've discussed.

As an apprentice working your day job of earning while you learn, there will come a time when your trainer will give you small tasks. For example, let's say you've taken an apprenticeship in the construction industry in carpentry.

Your trainer gives you the task of grabbing three boxes of nails out of the supply trailer. You already know where the supply trailer is, so you think, "Awesome, this is a task I can do!". So you head to the supply trailer to grab three boxes of nails, except when you get there.... there are about 25 boxes of nails of all different packaging.

Now you've got a choice: grab three random boxes of nails and head back to your trainer, or go home for the day because you don't want to make a mistake.

The correct answer is neither.

You shouldn't have been given that task without further clarifying instructions from the trainer. The trainer should have been more specific and clearly defined the type of nails, what side of the supply trailer they were stored on, and quite possibly what color the boxes the nails were packaged in.

There might be situations where working alone or performing tasks alone isn't going well in certain situations. Remember, within an apprenticeship - it takes two people to get the results that every apprenticeship is intended to deliver.

Those two people are you, the apprentice who is asking a lot of questions as you're there to learn, and the other, the trainer whose job it is to give you every detail of information to do your job correctly.

I promise you there will come a time in your apprenticeship when you will have the ability to work autonomously. It may take a year or more, but the day will come.

I'm sure you will have great trainers who are experts at what they teach as your success in an apprenticeship directly reflects how well you've been trained. Credentialed journey workers or trainers like myself take great pride in seeing the successes of apprentices.

A SECURE CAREER

I don't believe anyone would even consider an apprenticeship unless there was some "proof in the pudding" that apprenticeship works as intended, and that's a "get paid to learn environment" as the path to a lifelong career.

You might be thinking, "Just because this guy had success in an apprenticeship, how does that mean I'm going to be successful and have a long career and no college debt?".

The answer to your question isn't an exact science, but I hope at least this far into the book, you have a feeling that I know a bit about what I'm trying to tell you.

As plain as I can explain, apprentices need a regular influx of apprentices to close the gap between retirees and the replacement workforce. It's just that simple.

I might be using a weird analogy here, but I'm assuming that you are a high school or secondary school-age student, or you may be an adult who already has a career but is looking for a low-cost option to make a career change. It doesn't matter if you're male or female for this analogy.

The analogy is this: it takes buyers and sellers to drive the stock market, yes? What if there are no buyers? Will anyone complete a stock sale? What if someone wants to offload a poorly performing stock, but no one is buying?

It's defined as supply and demand. The demand for apprentices will not slow down at any point in the next decade or two, and that's why career-seeking students like yourself are in such an excellent position to capitalize on that demand and join an apprenticeship.

Apprentices are needed year after year and decade after decade to replace the people leaving the industries or sectors where apprenticeships are vital. Without apprentices to supply the in-demand occupations, things will get messy. Without an aging workforce that started their apprenticeships decades ago, there's no room for future apprentices.

This is another reason to consider an apprenticeship, and we will dive deeper into the growth rates of many industries and sectors we've previously touched on.

CAREER AND LEARNING OUTCOMES

Through my research for this book, when I was deciding what some of the most critical topics to tell you about, I continually ran into lists of why people choose apprenticeships as a career path instead of an expensive college degree. There are so many lists out there that I just decided to create my own list that I feel is more accurately explained as it's relative to the industries that need apprentices.

It's Free On The Job Training And Nearly Free Education. The on-the-job training is free for you, and your employer will pay you what the agreed-upon pay structure is. For example, the pay structure of many apprenticeships is to pay their apprentices an hourly wage plus a fringe benefits package that includes healthcare, dental, vision, vacation days, and more in some cases.

Most collective bargaining apprenticeships follow this pay structure; you are usually paid weekly. However, if you are in a private company's apprenticeship program, you may be on a bi-monthly pay structure, and your employer may match your retirement contributions.

You may get healthcare benefits as a free or shared cost and two to three weeks of paid time off or holiday pay. That would depend on the arrangement you've made with the employer.

When I say nearly free classroom education, it's a bit of a broad term. In most cases of collective bargaining apprenticeships, there is a small fee for each year of classroom training, and I will average it at USD 1000 or less each year. With so much technology in apprenticeship schools, much of that fee pays for the most up-to-date technical training tools, such as laptop computers or tablets to do your required school work.

In a non-collective bargaining apprenticeship school, you may be required to take a year or two of vocational schooling as an agreement for your apprenticeship, and vocational education may be nearing USD 10,000 for a two-year program.

You Will Gain Invaluable Skills And Experience. When you seek an apprenticeship, you desire a career occupation that trains you in one industry or sector. For example, suppose you want to work in the transportation industry. In that case, you may come out of your apprenticeship knowing how to completely disassemble and reassemble the engines that power the over-the-road trucks that many countries rely on for their supply and demand, or you may get into the field of logistics, which might be similar to an air traffic controller but for over the road trucks and at any given day and at any given time, you know where that truckload of bottled water is.

The skills and experience learned in an apprenticeship are worth every bit of your time and effort, as that is the foundation of your career.

Earn While You Learn. I can't stress this enough; I've touched on it many times in this book already. The one factor of an apprenticeship that should make it worth your interest is *you get paid to learn.*

Imagine you're approaching your graduation day from secondary school or high school, and you've already lined up an apprenticeship that will not only fast-track your career but also pay you a livable hourly wage or salary - and you could start this new apprenticeship the day after your commencement!

You would be four years ahead of your peers and earning income while they're still at college or university, hoping to get an entry-level job with their expensive degree!

Credentials That Follow You. Depending upon the industry or sector of your apprenticeship, your measure of success for an apprentice is earning the Journeyworker credential or a different certificate.

The natural progression of an apprenticeship is to fulfill your term of on-the-job training and classroom training. After that, you will validate you've learned the curriculum and the required skills to perform within that trade.

You're Ahead Of Your Peers. When you've chosen to take a different path than your peers and not enter college or university straight after commencement, you've made a great choice.

Understandably some young adults genuinely wish to go to college, and they may use the saying "to get the college experience." However, I'm pretty sure that if you had a crystal ball and could see into the future, you'd see some of those peers wishing they didn't have to make crippling student loan payments from their bank accounts for many years after they've left or graduated from college.

When you sign up for an apprenticeship, immediately on day one of your on-the-job training (that you're getting paid for), you are learning skills that will set you far apart from your peers.

You will have a four-year head start on those peers by gaining practical work experience in a specific field. Even if you don't feel that the apprenticeship was right for you and want to seek other opportunities, those years of practical experience will set you apart from other job seekers.

Out Of Pocket Costs. As I've mentioned earlier, most apprenticeships in the US have a small out-of-pocket cost for apprenticeship school. That will vary between the UK and Canada, and I believe in parts (if not all) of the UK, your education costs may be zero while you are in the apprenticeship. Costs for apprenticeship school in the US often vary by region, but I assure you it's a nominal fee that covers supplies, paper printing costs, and other general items that an adult learning center may require. Apprenticeship schools are not designed as for-profit institutions, and the yearly schooling cost (if any) is in place to cover the basic incidentals. It's safe to say that in the US, the typical apprenticeship yearly school cost is less than USD $1000 a year.

Canada may have some stipends available to offset the education cost for specific sectors, and depending on the industry and trade you enter for that apprenticeship, your education cost is manageable at around 500-1000 CAD yearly.

Learning From Experts. You cannot put a dollar value on the amount of information that credentialed people can pass along to apprentices. Those credentialed workers also went through an apprenticeship, and they remember what it's like to be an apprentice. It sometimes is a lot to juggle between life, working in your industry, and attending the required classroom instruction.

No Debt. Again, I keep pointing this out, and I cannot overlook reminding you that an apprenticeship provides the opportunity to have zero college debt as your portion of schooling tuition is very manageable and comparable to your income while working in your apprenticeship.

Imagine securing a four-year apprenticeship program on the day of high school commencement. You'll work during the day and get paid while you learn on the job. You will attend classes during the week, and those school hours would likely be paid working hours if the courses are during the workday. However, if those classes are after the workday, you likely wouldn't be paid to attend your apprentice school.

Four years pass, and you graduate from the apprenticeship and get your credentials. You meet up with some pals you knew during high school four years ago, and they go on and on about how great college was, and now they'll be starting to look for a job because they haven't been offered a job working in their field of study.

Wouldn't you be thinking to yourself how lucky you are that you've already been working for those four years they were away at college, and you don't have student loans burdening you?

We've discussed a lot of information in this chapter, and I hope I'm not leaving you with an overload of information that will be hard for you to process.

The key takeaways that you'll need to understand and figure out how they relate to your specific financial and career goals are:

• Do you have enough understanding about yourself to decide on a career path in one specific industry or sector?

• Do you have the desire and the resiliency to commit to an apprenticeship that will teach you everything you'll need to be successful in a long career?

• Would you forego an opportunity to have a "college experience" if it meant you could start building personal wealth immediately after your high school or secondary school commencement?

Would you jump at the opportunity to "earn while you learn" with on-the-job training?

Undoubtedly, an apprenticeship will be an excellent avenue for someone looking to jump-start their career in the workforce with little to no educational expense. Apprentices within the in-demand industries follow a pre-set program of earning on the job, schooling, and defined milestones that propel them through an apprenticeship program.

We've learned in this chapter that anyone who chooses to put their mind to the task can become an apprentice. We've talked about some great qualities of an apprentice, and that's not to say that a person must display those qualities to get accepted into an apprenticeship; a person just needs to show they want to learn those qualities.

We've also talked about what typically happens after you've completed all of your schooling and can work autonomously at your occupation and some of the benefits that go along with the trust an employer has for a credentialed worker. We've also discussed schooling and how an apprenticeship is set up to train the next generation of the workforce; thus, on-the-job training and the required classroom schooling are tailored as a benefit to the apprentice with minimal cost (if any) for the necessary education.

I often tell new apprentices I see in my classroom that time is the first thing they need to grasp as new apprentices. Time is of the essence in an apprenticeship, as all apprentices want to graduate from their programs just as quickly as they started, as they want to be making the complete pay packages that credentialed journey workers receive. An apprenticeship takes time to arrive at the finish line, and that's why I tell new apprentices to focus on their day job tasks and schooling, and the time will fly by quickly.

The next chapter details the in-demand industries with a severe shortage of replacement skilled workers for the foreseeable future. You'll be presented with many different sample occupations within those industries and sectors, and as you read through the next chapter, keep in mind that although you'll have to make a decision on which industry and occupation you'd like to pursue – all apprenticeships are set up to enable the success of the apprentice.

4

SUPPLY AND DEMAND

Many US, UK, and Canadian companies participate in and encourage apprenticeships as a career-building path. Some companies regularly hold apprentice outreach and recruiting events to find high school and secondary school-age applicants.

While some apprenticeships have an application process followed up by an interview process, other apprenticeship programs may require some basic aptitude testing as a condition of applying.

The basic aptitude testing is general testing that typically will be similar to the work you've done in your high school and most likely are from the subjects of basic English (or French in parts of Canada), basic math and arithmetic, and some basic reading tests.

For nearly all apprenticeships in the United States, a high school diploma or a general education diploma (GED) is a requirement. In addition, in the US, there is a minimum age requirement of eighteen years old to be eligible for an apprenticeship.

Just like within the UK and Canada, the US encourages men and women both to consider an apprenticeship regardless of skin tone, nationality, or any other discriminating factor. Apprenticeships in all three countries are open to anyone that wishes to have a career path and is willing to put in the time and effort. For most apprenticeships, however, you must be a citizen of the country where you seek the apprenticeship.

THE US INDUSTRIES

According to ApprenticeshipUSA, the United States' primary online resource for information about hundreds of available apprenticeships, the twelve significant industries are listed that support apprenticeships and actively recruit for those apprenticeships.

The US Industry List:

- Advanced Manufacturing
- Agriculture
- Construction
- Cybersecurity

- Education
- Energy
- Financial Services
- Healthcare
- Hospitality
- Information Technology
- Telecom
- Transportation

Within these industries, there is a long list of available apprenticeship programs for many high-demand occupations. I'll give you an example of just some career occupations that can start with an apprenticeship in each of the twelve US industries.

Advanced Manufacturing

- Aerospace Engineer
- Tool and Die Maker
- Mechanical Engineering Technician
- Mechatronics Technician
- Robotics Technician

Agriculture

- Farmers

- Ranchers
- Agricultural Management
- Plant and Soil Specialist
- Farm Equipment Service Technician

Construction

- Bricklayer
- Electrician
- Plumber
- Painter
- Sheet Metal Worker
- Boilermaker
- Elevator Constructor

Cybersecurity

- Cyber Analyst
- Cybersecurity Support Analyst
- Application Developer
- Cloud Operations Specialist

Education

- K-12 Teacher

- Teachers Aide
- Early Childhood/Pre-K Teacher
- Teaching Assistant

Energy

- Line Maintenance
- Electrician
- Gas-Main Fitter
- Water Treatment Operator

Financial Services

- General Insurance Associate
- Bank Teller
- Risk Consultant

Healthcare

- Dental Assistant
- Emergency Medical Technician/Paramedic
- Certified Nurse Aide
- Pharmacist Assistant

Hospitality

- Restaurant Manager

- Hotel/Lodging Manager
- Nutrition Care Specialist

Information Technology

- Computer Technician
- Software Development
- Cybersecurity Analyst
- Web Developer/Designer
- IT Project Manager

Telecom

- Telecommunications Tower Technician
- Wireless Technician
- Fiber Optic Technician
- IT Generalist
- Broadband Technician

Transportation

- Diesel Mechanic
- Airframe and Powerplant Mechanic
- Avionics Technician
- Truck Driver

Within each of these industries listed on the US Government's apprenticeship website is a plethora of information related to each career option within that industry.

The website also lists the competency-based framework that each apprenticeship is structured around, in addition to many industry-specific resources for you to be fully informed if you use this website in your research of apprenticeships and which one might be right for you.

Additionally, within many of the Industry categories on that website, there is also an "occupation finder" that is searchable by industry or specific occupation. You can search for a particular occupation within an industry or see a list of most occupations categorized by each sector.

Within the occupation finder, you will be pretty amazed to see that you can gather nearly all the information you'd need to understand what that occupation does, what some of the job conditions are, and what many daily tasks are.

Many of the occupations listed also will tell you how many months or years the related apprenticeship is expected to take and what the classroom instruction entails.

If you spend just a short time on the apprenticeship.gov website, you'll be much better informed about alternative career paths, which require little to no cost out of your pocket!

THE UK INDUSTRIES

The United Kingdom also does an excellent job of listing the major industries that support apprenticeships and the occupations that you might be interested in with those industries.

The website within the UK that seems to have provided the most exhaustive list of information is called The Apprenticeship Guide. Although I don't believe this website is sanctioned or sponsored by the UK Government, I still want to provide this information as it's too valuable not to share.

If you are a secondary school student in the UK and would like to access the website right now, you would need to point your web browser to:

Apprenticeshipguide.co.uk

So, let's dive into the UK industry list, and if you are curious about what apprenticeships might be available, I strongly urge you to visit the website and take lots of notes!!

The UK Industry List

- Agriculture, Environmental, and Animal Care
- Business and Administration
- Construction
- Creative, media, and the arts

- Customer service and retail
- Digital and ICT
- Energy
- Engineering and Electrical
- Financial services
- Hair and beauty
- Health and wellbeing
- Hospitality and travel
- Manufacturing, processing, and logistics
- Marine
- Public services
- Science and R&D
- Sport and fitness
- Vehicles and transportation

Just as occupations were listed under the US Industry categories, this UK website lists the fields in each industry. Below are some professions where you can secure an apprenticeship if you live in the UK.

Agriculture, Environmental, and Animal Care

- Abattoir Worker
- Agriculture Advisor

- Animal Trainer
- Arboriculturist
- Countryside Ranger
- Crop Technician
- Ecologist
- Environmental Practitioner
- Equine Groom
- Farrier, Fisher

Business and Administration

- Associate Project Manager
- Business Administrator
- Career Development Professional
- Coaching Professional, Conveyance Technician
- HR Consulting
- Internal Audit Professional
- Operational Research Specialist
- Paralegal
- Solicitor

Construction

- Advanced Carpentry

- Architectural Assistant
- Building Control Surveyor
- Civil Engineer
- Construction Site Supervisor
- Fire Safety Engineer
- Plumbing and Domestic Heating Technician
- Roofer
- Wireless Communications

Creative, Media, and the Arts

- Advertising and Media Executive
- Assistant Recording Technician
- Blacksmith
- Broadcasting
- Visual Effects

Customer Service and Retail

- Buyer/Merchandiser
- Butcher
- Fishmonger
- Funeral Director
- Retail

Digital and ICT

- Artificial Intelligence Data Specialist
- Audio/Visual Technician
- Cyber Security Technical
- Digital Marketing
- Geospatial Mapping

Energy

- Community Energy Specialist
- Electrical Power Engineer
- Gas Network Craftsperson
- Water Treatment Technician

Engineering and Electrical

- Aerospace Engineer
- Aerospace Software Development
- Aviation Maintenance Mechanic
- Electro-mechanical Engineer
- Embedded Electronic Systems Design and Development

Financial Services

- Accounting and Taxation Specialist
- Actuary

- Credit Controller
- Debt Advisor
- Mortgage Advisor
- Paraplanner

Hair and Beauty

- Advanced Hair Professional
- Beauty and Makeup
- Nail Services

Health and Wellbeing

- Adult Care Worker
- Clinical Practitioner
- Ambulance Support Worker
- Dental Technician
- Clinical Scientist
- Mammography

Hospitality and Travel

- Baker
- Chef
- Commercial Catering
- Hospitality Manager

- Maritime Caterer
- Senior Culinary Chef

Manufacturing, Processing, and Logistics

- Bespoke Tailor
- Brewer
- Delivery Manager
- Food and Drink Engineer
- Food Technologist
- Manufacturing Engineer
- Metal Fabricator

Marine

- Able Seafarer
- Boat-master
- Marina and Boatyard Operative
- Marine Engineer
- Maritime Mechanic

Public Services

- Academic Professional
- Church Minister
- Counter Fraud Investigator

- Custody and Detention Officer
- Fire Emergency and Security Systems

Science and R&D

- Animal Technology
- Bioinformatics Scientist
- Forensic Collection Investigator
- Laboratory Specialist
- Research Scientist

Sport and Fitness

- Advanced Sports Turf
- Personal Trainer
- Sports Coach

Vehicles and Transportation

- Air Traffic Controller
- Aviation Ground Handler
- Automotive Care Technician
- Highway Electrical Maintenance
- Network Operations

I want you to know that many more apprenticeships were listed for each industry, and had I listed every single one, I believe you probably would have dozed off a bit! I am impressed with how detailed The ApprentishipGuide website is and how much information is provided.

Within the specific apprenticeship pages, there are additional links you can view at your choosing and view the abundance of information. The additional information provided for each apprenticeship notes the duration of the program, the relevant school subjects, typical entry requirements into the apprenticeship, what level of achievement you will have upon completion, and the projected salary upon your completion of the apprenticeship.

The United Kingdom listing of apprenticeships is full of information on hundreds of occupations. I'm sure you will find it very useful to narrow down your choices for an apprenticeship!

THE CANADIAN SECTORS

Apprenticeships in Canada are no less in numbers than those in the US and UK, and Canadian apprenticeships are regulated and differentiated by a few classifications.

In full transparency, while researching this book, the Canadian apprenticeship information available is a bit of a rabbit hole of information. Canada has three territories and ten provinces, and it seems that each province is just a bit different than its neighboring province in how they approach apprenticeship programs.

Although the Canadian Government website provides information to investigate the available apprenticeships, it was tough to extrapolate a standardized data set and present it to you intelligently.

A non-profit organization called "The Working Centre" in Ontario has been a community development organization for over three decades as of 2023, and this organization provides a lengthy list of available trades with apprenticeship programs.

The Working Center has conflicting website information on whether the information is specific to Ontario only. However, I'm speculating that the information they provide is helpful for all provinces - as there are classifications of trades and apprentices that are the same throughout Canada.

No matter where I was looking for Canadian apprenticeship information, one obvious thing was that trade occupations and their subsequent apprenticeships are regulated in Canada, and the individual provinces administer that regulation.

The three regulated trade classifications are:

• Regulated - Compulsory

• Regulated - Voluntary

• Red Seal

Regulated - Compulsory. Explained as being illegal to work in the trade occupation without certification in that trade or registered as an apprentice with a specific employer.

Regulated - Voluntary. Provides an option to obtain certification to prove your skills and experience to a potential employer. In a Regulated - Voluntary trade, it is acceptable to perform the work without certification, and it is up to the individual employer whether they will require proof of experience.

Red Seal. The Red Seal trade employee has passed all available exams specific to that trade, and you will be recognized as having complete certifications. A Candian Red Seal trade is similar to the US licensed trade credentials. All provinces within Canada recognize the Red Seal trades. A Red Seal classification is transferrable between regions, and recertification to work in a different province will not be necessary.

Much like the US and UK have industries in which to develop and maintain apprenticeship programs, Canada has four sectors.

The Canadian Sectors list:

- Construction
- Industrial
- Motive Power
- Services

Canada has just as many occupational opportunities for skilled workers and apprentices as the US and the UK. The sampling of occupations listed below for each sector may be classified as a Compulsory Trade or a Red Seal Trade. I will make those indications by abbreviating in parenthesis (RST) for Red Seal Trade and (CT) for Compulsory Trade. Trades listed that have both (RST) and (CT) behind them have dual classification.

Construction

- Architectural Glass and Metal Technician (CT)

- Brick and Stone Mason (CT)

- Cement (Concrete) Finisher

- Construction Boilermaker (CT)

- Drywall Finisher and Plasterer

- Drywall, Acoustic, and Lathing Applicator (CT)

- Electrician — Construction and Maintenance (RST)

- Electrician — Domestic and Rural (RST)

- General Carpenter (CT)

- Heat and Frost Insulator (CT)

- Heavy Equipment Operator — Dozer

- Hoisting Engineer — Mobile Crane Operator 1 & 2 (RST)

- Plumber (RST) (CT)

- Powerline Technician (CT)
- Refrigeration and Air Conditioning Systems Mechanic (RST) (CT)
- Sheet Metal Worker (RST) (CT)
- Steamfitter (RST) (CT)

Industrial

- Bearings Mechanic
- Blacksmith
- Cabinetmaker (CT)
- Draftsperson — Mechanical
- Electrical Control (Machine) Builder
- Fitter — Assembler (Motor Assembly)
- Industrial Electrician (CT)
- Industrial Mechanic Millwright (CT)
- Metal Fabricator (Fitter) (CT)
- Pressure Systems Welder
- Surface Blaster, Tool and Die Maker (CT)
- Tractor-Trailer Commercial Driver
- Water Well Driller
- Welder (CT)

Motive Power

- Agricultural Equipment Technician (CT)
- Alignment and Brakes Technician (RST)
- Auto Body and Collision Damage Repairer (RST) (CT)
- Fuel and Electrical Systems Technician (RST)
- Heavy Duty Equipment Technician (CT)
- Marine Engine Technician
- Recreation Vehicle Technician (CT)
- Truck-Trailer Service Technician (RST) (CT)

Services

- Aboriginal Child Development Practitioner
- Appliance Service Technician (CT)
- Arborist
- Chef
- Child and Youth Worker
- Child Development Practitioner
- Electronic Service Technician
- Hairstylist (RST) (CT)
- Horticultural Technician (CT)
- Micro Electronics Manufacturer

- Network Cabling Specialist

- Retail Meat Cutter

- Special Events Coordinator

Although the list of trades with apprenticeships in Canada has a few regulated trade classifications, that should not deter you from seeking your apprenticeship.

Additionally, remember that an apprenticeship is your stepping stone to a lifelong career and is a wise financial decision that will propel you to living a student loan debt-free life!

Whoa! That was a ton of information we have covered in this chapter. I have memories of many years ago when I was in middle school when I might have been told my "answers were vague" or I "wasn't providing enough information" on my class work.

I took that to heart, and when I commit to providing information, I tend to go all out.

As you've read, the United States, the United Kingdom, and Canada are committed to providing apprenticeship opportunities to anyone like you searching for the right career opportunities that don't require an expensive four-year degree from a college. I can't stress enough that the options are out there, and most of the apprenticeships available have information on the Internet.

The amount of information I've provided in this chapter might seem overwhelming to you, and if so - take the research part of it slow. This book highlights information I've collected over the years and some of the latest updated information about in-demand industries.

Once you start researching from the comfort of your computer or laptop, I assure you that you will create a system that allows for good organization of your notes.

5

GAINING SKILLS, NOT DEBT

QUESTIONING DECISIONS

According to Gates Foundation research, more and more new college students are heavily questioning whether a college degree will provide a financially positive return on their investment, and those that were surveyed commented that had they known how easily they could have transitioned from secondary school into an apprenticeship, they likely would have done some research.

Additional studies polled adults aged 18-35 who either opted not to seek college after high school commencement or dropped out of college altogether.

The data from those studies suggested that in that age bracket, adults were sure that the cost of the four-year degree far outweighed the potential income benefits within fifteen years after graduating college. Those adults did not see the value in paying for a college degree without a solid sense of reassurance that the college degree would lead to high-salary working positions.

Overall in that age group of 18-35, over 40% of the people polled didn't want the expensive college debt that comes shortly after graduation.

A recent Forbes Magazine article released data from a poll they conducted. In that poll, respondents were asked the question of "what types of additional education and training after high school are the best value".

Here are the respondent's answers:

- On-the-job training - 74%

- A course to receive licensure - 70%

- A course that provides professional certification(s) 68%

- A course that provides a verified certificate - 67%

- A 2-year college degree - 61%

- A 4-year university or college degree - 60%

Many students on the cusp of graduating or even entering their last year of high school are already questioning if college is the only way. There is a sentiment in some areas of the US where high school-age students believe their high schools are dropping the ball on providing factual information regarding the college process and the anxiety that sets in on many recent college graduates that struggle to find the right job, all while having hefty student loan payments.

Many of those same students feel like their high schools weren't preparing them for life after high school, and some students have already decided that there may be other ways to prove their worth to a company to obtain a steady income.

The Forbes article concludes with a stark glimpse into the new way that college-ready young adults are thinking, and that was shown when they are given a task to list fifteen priorities they felt were important to them to achieve in a few years, "Getting a college degree" was pushed down the list by priorities such as "positive emotional health" and "spending time with family."

In fact, "getting a college degree" ranked at the bottom of the list.

The good part about all the information above for you is that if secondary schools and colleges possibly start to lose their grip on the "college is the only way" mindset, that means more apprenticeships will be surfacing in the coming decade, as there will be greater demand for low cost, skills building educational paths that young adults can be proud to say they've made a choice to do.

A blog written some years ago for a Michigan Construction website gathered data on what the sentiment was on the rising cost costs of college topics. The blog notes that in 1980, the average cost of college tuition was roughly $2,100. That same four-year program, with adjustments for inflation and the high cost of almost everything else, would average to around $96,000 today.

That's why apprenticeships should be talked about in every high school, secondary school, preparatory school, and home school in every part of the world.

Here are some talking points about apprenticeships that I don't think I've provided you with yet:

• The average length of an apprenticeship from start to finish is 3.5 years (heavily dependent on the industry you choose).

• The yearly income for apprentices in some industries nearly surpasses that of a four-year college graduate just starting their working career.

• The out-of-pocket education costs for an apprenticeship are tax deductible in the US as a work-related expense.

• Recent surveys of employers indicate that over 90% of those employers agreed that apprentices brought value to their businesses.

• As an apprentice, you will get a yearly raise that can be as much as 15% year over year as you progress through a program. (Industry dependent).

I've known many career-change people who've left their corporate jobs in the rearview mirror and signed up for an apprenticeship as they don't want to put themselves into college debt again, yet they desire a new career. An apprenticeship will provide education and training both on the job and hands-on in the classroom, and it also will provide a strong career path for years to come.

As I said before, I believe there is a need for college seekers. There are simply some careers and occupations that can only be had through traditional college, and those folks manage to figure out their careers and how to pay their student loans if they acquire them. I want people like yourself to be educated on all options, including college if that is your choice - and then you can decide.

I'll close out this topic in this chapter with more facts and figures for you.

This comparison of the cost between a Bachelor's degree and an apprenticeship is somewhat eye-opening:

• An average apprenticeship educational cost is $2,500 - USD 5,000 over the term of the apprenticeship depending on the industry, type, and whether it's a union apprenticeship or private company apprenticeship.

• The average four-year cost of a Bachelor's degree is USD $127,000.

• More than 20% of Bachelor's degree holders owe more than $50,000 to their student loans, and 6-8% of those people owe more than $100,000.

• The average 20-year net income for occupations started in apprenticeship is $441,000 more than the 20-year average for Bachelor's degree holders.

- The average savings for an apprenticeship student education cost is USD $114,000 less than a Bachelor's degree student.

EARN WHILE YOU LEARN

I've been telling you about this for many chapters in this book, and now we will get into the earn while you learn to model in detail.

If you happened to be randomly walking through the US Government Department of Labor on any random day and asked someone in that organization what an apprenticeship was, they likely would reply to you, "an apprenticeship is an arrangement in which you get hands-on training, technical instruction, AND a paycheck, all at the same time."

Although the Department of Labor (DOL) has nothing to do with the regular payroll for apprentices, they set the standards for the earn-while-you-learn model and heavily monitor most of the larger apprenticeship organizations in the US.

Remember when I said that AppsForYou was starting its apprenticeship and needed to get its apprenticeship plan submitted and approved? It would likely have been the US Department of Labor or a state-level equivalent that would have signed off.

The website CareerVision tracks many of the US Bureau of Labor Statistics bulletins as they are released, and a recent report by CareerVision stated this:

• The US Bureau of Labor Statistics projects employment in many occupations with apprenticeships will grow *at least as fast* (*if not faster*) than the average of all occupations over the next decade (2018-2028).

• Earnings for many top occupations with apprenticeships are well above the median annual wage of $38,640 for all fields in 2018. (I'll stress that these are median - meaning middle of the pack estimates).

• The DOL counted approximately 585,000 active apprentices in more than 23,000 registered programs in 2018.

Apprenticeships are generally on the rise, and the interest in apprenticeships is growing (albeit slowly), as I've said before.

You may be wondering if, in this chapter, I'll be giving you a breakdown of the dollars and cents that an apprentice can earn if you are in this industry or if you're in a particular sector, and my short answer is no, as it's just not possible to gather all of that data accurately due to the number of different apprenticeship programs in the US, UK, and Canada.

What I can give you, however, is the average annual wage for a few in-demand and highly sought-after apprenticeships in the US based on available data.

In 2018 the median apprentice wages at the mid-point of their apprenticeship in USD were:

- Carpenter - $47,000

- Construction Laborer - $39,800

- Electrical Power Line Install and Repair - $59,910

- Electrician - $55,190

- Heavy Equipment Operator - $48,630

- Plumber, Pipefitter, Steamfitter - $53,910

- Sheet Metal Worker - $48,650

The list above is a bit subjective, in my opinion. So many factors affect these numbers, and I would tell you don't let these discourage you if you feel that an apprenticeship wouldn't be worth it based on these numbers. These numbers indicate the halfway point through an apprenticeship and are roughly 40-50% of full journey worker pay.

I'm speculating that this median wage list may have used non-collective bargaining (non-union) as an example, which would circle us back to the union or non-union thing. Remember when I had said if you were an apprentice for a private company-sponsored apprenticeship, you'd more than likely be negotiating your pay increases, benefits, etc.?

In a collective bargaining apprenticeship, those numbers above will be considerably higher as you start your last few years of apprenticeship once you factor in your pay rate plus your benefits package, including health care, etc.

Most apprenticeships follow a similar structure of pay regardless if they are collective bargaining or not.

If you are an apprentice and just starting, you should expect to get paid a certain percentage of what the credentialed or licensed workers are receiving. This is called "stepped pay" and is not to be confused with "merit pay," which we discussed earlier in the book.

In an apprenticeship stepped pay system, the apprentice typically starts in a program with approximately 35-45% of what the skilled and experienced workers make. Then, as you progress through the program, a typical yearly or bi-yearly automatic pay increase will occur to the next percentage (as set forth by the apprenticeship).

Typically the stepped pay increases by 10-15% yearly after your first year of apprenticeship, and depending on the length of your training, you will earn about 85-90% of what the experienced workers are making.

The last percentage bump is saved for when you are a credentialed or licensed worker, and that is by design. The idea is that every year of a multi-year apprenticeship program, you deserve an increase in pay just by nature of your commitment to an apprenticeship program. Still, the percentage held back until you've been licensed or credentialed is just a little extra motivation to complete your program on time and study hard for your skills exams.

If I could survive a stepped pay system in my five-year apprenticeship program, you can too.

LENGTH OF AN APPRENTICESHIP PROGRAM

The length of an apprenticeship program is an important topic to talk about here, as I'm pretty sure it will be a big question you might have. So I will preface this subtopic by saying again that all apprenticeships are not equal, they are all not regulated or designed the same way, and when you are doing your research, you may run into information that completely conflicts with what I'm telling you and if that's the case I wholeheartedly apologize.

With the tens of thousands of apprenticeships in the US, the seemingly same amount in Canada and the UK, there was no possibility that I could provide details about every apprenticeship out there - it just wouldn't be possible to get that in-depth. If I went on and on giving you the information on every apprenticeship available, this book would have been a ten-volume set.

The timeline to complete an apprenticeship relies on the program sponsor and whatever they determine as appropriate. As you start diving into the internet to research, you will want to pay keen attention to the apprenticeship listing, details, and descriptions and take notes. In particular, you should be paying close attention to how the structure of pay is explained, the projected timeline from start to finish of the program, and whether it's an earn-while-you-learn apprenticeship or is structured like an internship where the training is just designed to give you practical experience.

Multiple US industries follow the same model as some of the most popular construction apprenticeships in the US. Hence, it's safe to say if it's a US federally sponsored apprenticeship - it is a multiyear apprenticeship. So if you are interested in the construction industry, you should plan for a multiyear apprenticeship in the US of anywhere between 3 and 5 years.

Many company-sponsored apprenticeships will follow the company guidelines as per their approval for an apprenticeship. Still, those tend to be shorter as the classroom portion of some company-sponsored apprenticeships won't be nearly as hands-on.

For many US Registered apprenticeships, the required on-the-job training hours and required schooling hours are very similar between the industries and have no differences if an apprentice is in a collective bargaining apprenticeship or a company-sponsored non-collective bargaining apprenticeship.

The requirements for many US registered apprenticeships average 1800 hours of on-the-job training per year, and 144 hours of related per-year technical instruction hours, primarily received in a classroom or a hands-on learning environment taught by registered experts in their field.

The apprenticeship school schedule is typically 1 to 2 days or evenings a week, which may be during or after the work day from late afternoon into the evening. Most in-school training classes are 3.5 - 4.5 hours long and include breaks between learning modules.

In most cases of apprenticeship, the cost of the education is minimal to the apprentice, and the remainder may be paid by some of the employers that support that apprenticeship.

Many apprenticeships manage and run their training centers, while some apprenticeships either rent space in a local community building or maybe even a local vocational center or community college. It is widespread for Federally registered apprenticeships to have full-time staff working within these training centers, as they are considered post-secondary education institutions just as colleges and universities are.

If a training center for an apprenticeship does indeed have its own facility, the buildings are laid out with you, the apprentice, in mind. They are technologically advanced, utilizing web cameras and video conferencing capabilities; some are even set up so instructors can teach remotely via a web camera and instruct people across a large geographical area who may not be able to be in the classroom.

These training centers also have things you'd typically see on a college campus, such as in-house meals if equipped to serve students. In addition, many have very nice lounge areas, vending services, and comfortable furniture to relax or socialize, and many apprenticeship training centers pride themselves on having an institution that feels just like a college campus - without the incredibly high price tag.

Overall, the look and feel of an apprenticeship training center, whether as a standalone building or as part of another higher education institutions campus, very much looks and feels like a campus where adults are there to learn and support one another, just as is the feel of some of the most prominent college campuses.

When you become an apprentice, you become an adult learner and are surrounded by like-minded adults who are all there for the same reason - to advance their careers without the high cost of college.

APPRENTICESHIP AS THE NEW COLLEGE DEGREE

Recent information released in the last quarter of 2022 implies that college graduates who have been in the workforce for a decade or more are trending toward a career shift. The driving factor for 39% of those in the surveyed workforce indicates the primary reason for the career-shift mindset is that workers are unhappy with their salaries. People surveyed also indicated they don't feel an equal rise in wage or pay structures, which mirrors the rising cost of business. The increasing cost of doing business equals rising profits for employers, and many in the workforce feel under-compensated as company profits continue to sustain or grow.

Industry experts cannot confirm or deny the sentiment on whether an apprenticeship could be considered "the new college degree." Still, CNBC reports that due to the heightened demand for workers, the continually rising cost of tuition, and the subsequent skyrocketing student loan burden is what's driving more students to choose career-connected pathways over four-year colleges (Dickler, 2023). As a college dropout and a former apprentice, I can undeniably say that if more career-ready high school students understood the value of an apprenticeship, the US would likely enter into an industrial revolution updated for today's technological advancements.

Data also suggests that 44% of those surveyed about career happiness have already made plans for their next career endeavor.

Although interest in joining an apprenticeship immediately after commencement from high school or secondary school is on the rise, the shortfall in the need for a workforce that consistently shrinks year over year is not ending any time soon. The manufacturing of goods, the technology it takes to produce just about any tangible item, and the technologically creative minds it takes to design those products are all gaining ground.

The discussion of apprenticeship over college is also gaining ground, albeit very slowly, but young adults and career shifters are starting to listen. As a result, many in-demand industries are retaining consulting firms to perform studies that can project who the ideal candidates are to replace the existing aging workforce, and the results are a bit surprising.

News Nation Now reports that many college graduates who seemingly picked a field of study that showed growth potential during their four-year degree program are now considering the degree they chose as the wrong choice. (Dorn, 2023).

The study states that these standard degree fields are seeing the most significant shift into a new career path that includes an apprenticeship to gain the skills and education needed to effectively transfer into a new career.

The survey reports the percentages of degreed adults who would now choose an apprenticeship over their original degree as:

- 48% in Humanities/Arts

- 46% in Social/Behavioral Sciences

- 40% in education

- 37% in Business Management

A 2016 LinkedIn report further identifies that an average of 47% of people within the UK and the US secretly hope a career change will be in their future. That number is staggering, but even more staggering is that 66% of the 47% surveyed were classified as millennials.

Understandably, people are continuing to stay in their careers due to the uncertainty of what a shift to a new job or even an unfamiliar career change into an apprenticeship will look like for them.

When I speak on the subject of apprenticeship to groups or even talking to individuals who are just picking my brain for information, the one point I always leave them with is this: apprenticeships have been around for thousands of years in one form or another, and apprenticeships are certainly not a new, untested idea or pathway to a sustainable career.

Within the US, UK, and Canada, apprenticeships have transformed into the earn-while-you-learn format they are today. Considering the stepped pay structure of an apprenticeship that nearly outweighs the average starting salary for a college graduate with a four-year degree, apprenticeships are a far better option in the long run than taking four years of college debt into the working world with you to start your career.

Be The Voice That "College Is Not The Only Way" To Career Success!

How well-versed are you in the world of apprenticeships? If your answer leans towards the "not much" side, you're not alone. While traditional higher education provides a valuable foundation, the focus often hovers over academic pursuits, leaving the subject of apprenticeships largely unexplored.

Embarking on an apprenticeship not only equips you with lifelong skills but also guarantees a stable income and a sustainable career. However, the key to unlocking this future lies in having the right information at your fingertips. Drawing from my own career, my mission is to share insights that empower you to hone your skills and discover your true calling.

Think about the countless teens navigating the maze of career options, just like you. Your assistance in spreading the word about apprenticeships can make a world of difference, and it won't demand much of your time—less than a few minutes, all from the comfort of your home!

The pathway to passing along this invaluable guidance is as straightforward as sharing a brief review online. By expressing your thoughts about this book, particularly on platforms like Amazon, you're not just helping yourself, but ensuring that other young adults will stumble upon this wealth of information about this valuable and undeniable career opportunity that is rarely mentioned in high schools.

The power of book reviews cannot be overstated—they are the validation that guides us to the answers we seek. A few sentences from you could inspire a fellow teenager to explore this introduction into apprenticeships, just as you may have wished for guidance when exploring alternatives to college in high school.

By leaving a review of this book on Amazon, you'll make sure other young people find it and discover the full range of possibilities for their future.

Your support is the catalyst for change. Take a moment to leave a review, and let's continue on this journey towards career success and financial freedom.

Your voice matters more than you think!

Scan the QR code to leave an honest Amazon review.

6
APPRENTICE CAREER DEVELOPMENT

STARTING AT THE BOTTOM

The development of a skilled labor career doesn't happen overnight, and no matter how much you daydream or define a path you want your career to take, a simple hiccup in the plan can send a career into a spiral. The key is; being able to manage that hiccup. As we all are big dreamers, I'm sure I'm not alone in thinking everyone (including you someday) will think about what the "top" of your career looks like.

For lawyers, maybe it's becoming a State's Attorney; for Doctors, perhaps it's being named Department Lead in a well-known medical center. For a politician, maybe it's becoming President or Prime Minister. Everyone has a different idea of "development," and my career development took many years for me to feel I was carving out a successful career from an apprenticeship. I am now in the last stages of my career, and I passionately educate, observe and engage with apprentices on how to push their careers in the right direction so they can achieve the fruits of their labor.

As an apprentice, I had very little knowledge of the stages of a career within any occupation in my industry. I had never asked any other trades workers around me how they carved out their careers and if they could tell me some milestones.

What I did do, though, is keep mental notes throughout my working career of the events that led my career in a new direction multiple times. I'll share more about that later in this chapter.

Career planning guides will detail many types of career development traits and qualities, and for the most part, I agree with them. However, what is even better for you to learn and understand is that a lot of career development could be explained as coming from within yourself.

When you become an apprentice, there will be tons of information coming at you that you might not understand, and frankly, it might make you nervous or anxious and sometimes frustrated. This is natural, and only because you're new to an apprenticeship program, and this might be a whole new world for you. This might be your first inclination for a career development trait called "Self Awareness."

When you are self-aware, you understand that you might not know everything even though you're trying your hardest to learn everything. Being self-aware also means you shouldn't put undue stress on yourself while attempting to learn new skills and ideas.

Suppose you were in an Information Technology apprenticeship, and the trainer you were working with asked you to run some cable through the wall and use the left-handed cable stretching tool. Would you ask another person on the project where the left-handed cable stretching tool was? Maybe, but I'm sure you'd get a pretty comical response from the person you asked for the device.

Self-awareness is also understanding your limitations and when to ask for help if you've hit a limit. For example, if someone had asked you to find a left-handed cable stretching tool and you've never heard that term, the right thing to do is to ask for clarification on the device. What does it look like? Is it big or little? Where could you find the tool if you went to look for it?

It's questions like that set an apprentice apart from the pack. By asking questions, it shows that you're not willing just to run off and spend hours looking for a tool you've never heard of; it's that you'd instead be informed and have a basis of information to go on when completing a task like finding a tool.

LEARNING ON THE JOB

Apprentices are on the job and in the classroom to learn. If you're not learning, what's the point? It's your job to help and foster your learning abilities, and what is the absolute best way to learn? Ask questions. Asking questions is also one of the most important things you can do on a job as an apprentice, in addition to asking questions in the classroom. The more knowledge you have about your occupation, the better you will be.

Apprenticeships require very few qualifications for entrance other than, at minimum, a high school diploma or a general education diploma in the United States. That means you can apply for an apprenticeship in a field you might not know anything about. (Hopefully, you've researched before the application process and at least understand the occupation within that industry).

Because most apprenticeships have very few requirements for acceptance other than maybe a general aptitude for the industry, your career development starts on day one through everything you learn on the job. You might find that as you are progressing through your apprentice school that things aren't making sense between what you learn on the job and what you learn in school, but I assure you the day will come when a proverbial lightbulb will go off above your head, and things will start to click.

You might see a particular piece of equipment installed in a certain way on the job, and then you'll remember that you had just talked about that a week or two before in the classroom. So that also is career development.

Learning something new every day is a highly attainable goal for an apprentice.

Coursera, the professional development website, lists some strategic career development objectives and abilities as:

- Developing a new skill set
- Developing your workplace skills
- Taking up leadership responsibilities
- Expanding your professional network
- Gaining professional credentials
- Finding ways to deepen job satisfaction
- Taking relevant courses to further your education.

This list might seem like a long list of things you'll need to do to help your career development, but it isn't. Most of these items you might be able to check off within a month or two of starting your apprenticeship, and all of these career development objectives are very attainable within the first few years after you complete your training.

I'll give examples from the above list of how I didn't even know I was having "career development" as it seemed like the everyday job-related things I was doing.

Developing a new skill set. Every day I worked in the field, whether on a bustling construction site or in a quiet home of a customer, I learned new skills. Large construction projects require different materials, different ways of doing regular tasks, and more distractions than usual due to heavy equipment and more trades on the project. Working autonomously in a customer's house requires different skills than working on busy construction projects. I've always thought that if I'm in someone else's home working to fix the issue I was called there to improve, I need to be overly aware that I am in their space, and I don't want there to be a trace that I was even there.

Taking up leadership responsibilities. The natural career progression for an apprentice can look like this: you start your career as an apprentice learning from others. After a certain period, you'll prove your knowledge and skills and become credentialed or licensed; now, you can work independently. You'll work independently for a while, and then you'll probably get the opportunity to be an on-the-job trainer for new apprentices. Guess what? That's leadership. You've proven yourself to be worthwhile doing your job, and now your employer is allowing you to train new apprentices that are new, just like you were one day a long time ago.

Gaining professional credentials. You already know the industry I work in is construction, and I've been in this fast-paced industry for over 26 years. This industry has brought me many years of steady work with great pay and benefits, and I couldn't imagine having a career in any other industry. I became licensed in my trade after my five-year apprenticeship and furthered those credentials when I became "Master" licensed a handful of years later. Later in my career, I again became "Master" credentialed, this time in an adjoining state to my own.

In the construction industry, there are licensed trades and unlicensed trades - and that's not meant to be taken as "important" trades or "unimportant" trades, as all skilled trades are essential. For example, take just a minute to look around the house or building you may be sitting in and reading this book. There likely were 8 to 10 different trades involved in constructing that building, and every skilled trade that built that structure was equally as important as the others.

Some trades are licensed, and some are not. I've explained in a previous chapter that licensed or unlicensed does not mean important or unimportant; it's just that some trades, such as Plumbing, Electrical, and Gas Fitting, have an element of danger or disease to them if installed incorrectly, hence the need for licensure that proves the competency of the skilled worker. Licenses are regulated at the state level within the US. In the UK, they have a "competent person" designation, verifying the worker has proven knowledge and skills.

As a licensed tradesperson, I am responsible for ensuring the licenses I keep are up to date and that all of my required ongoing education requirements are met to renew my licenses. If I can't get my licenses renewed, I can't work. Plumbers, Electricians, and Gas Fitters in the US and Canada can get a license or a certification using new technology in their field, which is a big part of your career development and why you would effectively make yourself very attractive to a new employer. The more credentials you have, the more desirable you are to an employer looking for a skilled worker to perform specific tasks - and since I had just proven my skills to receive that new credential, I became more valuable to my employer. Depending on the industry of your apprenticeship, this might also become a familiar situation to you.

Whether it's the construction industry or any other, there is no bad outcome from leveling up your credentials. Your credentials are like a resume or a CV; the more certifications you can have - the more value you can bring to a job site or an employer.

Finding other ways to deepen job satisfaction. I will preface my explanation by saying I've never been dissatisfied with my occupation. Have things always gone perfectly smoothly? No. Would I choose this career again if I had to make a choice? Yes.

Job satisfaction is also a somewhat subjective term, like career development. I have job satisfaction nearly every day when I see a customer smile at the work that I've done or when I engage my boss in a conversation and for a few minutes, he can slip away from the stresses of running a business, and we can talk about the latest superstar or the sports scores from the day before.

After a quarter century of working within a steadily growing industry, I genuinely believe job satisfaction is what you make of your situation. I love a challenge, and in the occupation within construction I'm in - it's sometimes a challenge by the hour. There's always some aspect of my work that needs attending to, whether it is returning customer phone calls, purchasing materials, or solving problems like how to fit a square peg into a round hole. *I love to work, so that is my job satisfaction.* I love to sit down and write when my day job work is done, so that's my retreat from a busy workday and how I always keep myself satisfied. I like to help people during the day fix their problems on a construction site or in their homes, and after work, I want to write books that might help people improve an issue or solve a problem they might be having.

When you get accepted into an apprenticeship, you will figure out very quickly what you enjoy and what you don't enjoy. For example, maybe your apprenticeship job requires you to wake up at 5 am and be to work by 6 am, but you were used to getting up at 9 am before the apprenticeship started, and it's tough for you to even think about getting up at 5 to go to work. But, on the other hand, if your apprenticeship job required you to be present at 5 am on the day you got your paycheck, would you stay in bed, or would you show up at 4:30 am to be sure you didn't miss your pay envelope?

That's how I look at things, and I'm sure you will as well once you get into your apprenticeship. Without a doubt, you will probably be questioning your decision to enter an apprenticeship at some point, as nothing is rainbows and roses every minute of every day, especially in a new environment like an apprenticeship. However, you must remember certain things you must do to get to the things that mean the most. You likely will understand once in your apprenticeship that struggling through the hard days will pay off, which is the reward for a skilled trade or similar skilled occupation. The paycheck means a great deal to me, so if I have to work hard during the week to ensure that I get that regular paycheck, that is what I need to do, and I'm satisfied with the deal.

7

FROM APPRENTICE TO FINANCIAL FREEDOM

You might be wondering what a chapter about finances is doing in this book as you probably would tell me something like, "I've been working since I was in my middle teens, and I've saved a lot of money." Well, that may be true, and congratulations, you've learned the one skill that many people don't know how to do - and that is to save money.

I discuss the topic of finances frequently when I'm teaching a new batch of apprentices. My motive behind the topic and one of my reasons for wanting to drive this topic into their brains are that it's a very slippery slope to go from being a young adult with a restaurant job or a petrol station job into an industry and career where the pay increases are regular, and the pay is excellent.

I've seen numerous apprentices through the years I've been teaching nearly go into bankruptcy because they didn't make financially smart and intelligent decisions as their apprentice pay increased year over year. When I taught classes about money and budgeting to apprentices, they were titled "Financial Literacy," which is what it boils down to. Being financially literate in a career that increases your pay 10-15% year after year until you're nearing the six-figure range is not something everyone can master right off the bat.

I've seen apprentices making about 80% of their top pay tier get so excited to have money in their pocket and in the bank go out and buy sixty or seventy thousand dollar trucks "because they can afford it" (their words). No one should tell them they can't afford it because they likely have the money to make the monthly payment on that truck, but what if the economy crashes in a year after buying that truck and the work dries up for a month or two? What if you randomly catch a virus that lands you in the hospital for two to three weeks, and you can't work? What if?

That's why with every new batch of apprentices that come through my class, we spend at least 4 hours on this topic. TO HAVE THE MONEY TO SPEND is exponentially different from HAVE TO SPEND THE MONEY, and that's the basis of my discussion.

DEFINING YOUR FINANCIAL FREEDOM

Financial freedom is a bit of a subjective term. My financial freedom probably looks quite different from your financial freedom because everyone's definition of financial freedom comes from within. People everywhere have differing explanations of what being rich or poor means, and no two people are probably in the same financial situation. The value of the US dollar has fluctuated enough over the past hundred years that it's anyone's guess whether the dollar we save for retirement today will still be worth a dollar when we get there.

MoneyFit.org defines Financial Freedom as: Financial freedom usually means having enough savings, financial investments, and cash on hand to afford the kind of life we deserve for ourselves and our families. (Christensen, 2023).

Money managers, financial experts, and people whose job is to tell those who don't work in the finance industry what we should be doing with our money may not see the entire big picture regarding financial freedom. Although I agree with the MoneyFit.org definition, it does not apply to everyone from every walk of life.

This is why you need to define your financial freedom.

Maybe your financial freedom is a weekend trip to New York City or Paris to stay at five-star hotels and eat at all the fine restaurants listed in the Michelin Guide. If so, that's great!

Your financial freedom might include getting your hot air balloon private pilot's license and flying your family around to watch the world from 1500 feet above the Earth.

Maybe your financial freedom is never having to worry about how to cover your expenses from week to week or even just simply having cash in your pocket regularly. These two things were my definition of financial freedom when I was in my early twenties, on my own and struggling to gain a foothold on adulting.

Apprenticeship Pay

Although the amount of time from when you start your apprenticeship to when you become a fully skilled and credentialed journey worker might seem initially like waiting for the next millennium, I assure you that in just a few years after your apprenticeship is over you will think it went as quick as the blink of an eye.

When you start as an apprentice, you'll earn a paycheck through the earn-while-you-learn job training model. However, when you are new to a trade or an occupation, you have limited knowledge of the job requirements, and your skills are minimal. So, naturally, your pay structure would be minimal as well. However, the beginning minimum pay structure is still a healthy yearly income.

An apprenticeship typically is an incremental stepped earning system. In year one of your apprenticeship, you're at the base wage. In year two, you'll likely be at the base plus a certain percentage of the journey worker's earnings.

In year three (if your apprenticeship flows into a third year and beyond), you'd be at the base wage, plus your second-year percentage increase, plus you'd now be entitled to a third-year stepped wage increase. This stepped pay system is in place in many construction apprenticeships, and the model works well.

That's not to say that apprentices new to a career don't deserve big money right from the start; it's just a fair and even pay system that advances as you advance through a program and brings more value each year of your apprenticeship. You'll be gaining skills on the job and knowledge in the classroom of your selected occupation, and it just makes the most sense to have a skills-based earning system in place.

Once you finally reach the end of your apprenticeship, you may quickly be making a six-figure yearly income if you were to calculate your fringe benefits as part of your annual income.

The last two years of my apprenticeship are when I saw the earnings of my skilled trade occupation start to climb. In these years, my definition of financial freedom became very clear. I was under 32 years old in those last few years of my apprenticeship. Although my wife and I had already started a family, the wage increases each of those last two years relieved me that my weekly pay was far outweighing the weekly budget my wife and I had set for ourselves. Finally, we had some breathing room and could start thinking about small non-necessity expenses.

As an apprentice, it will be in your best interest to learn about debt-to-income ratios, which are the number one factor a home purchase is based upon in the US. At some point during your apprenticeship, you might want to purchase a house to start your family. In that case, it will be in your best interest to have some money in the bank as mortgage lenders in the US look at your available funds as proof of worthiness for a home mortgage.

Most credit reporting agencies also use the debt-to-income ratio in their algorithms when calculating whether someone is a risk for a loan. I ran just a few quick calculations to see what an average first-year apprentice's yearly income is against an average 12-month rent or mortgage, and this is what I came up with. You can use this quick calculation if you're doing some math in your decision-making process on what the apprentice pay structure might mean to you based on your expenses.

If an apprentice made USD 40,000 in their first year of apprenticeship and their monthly expenses were USD 1,500, their DTI (debt to income) ratio would be at a 40% mark which is considered a bit high.

If an apprentice made USD 65,000 in their second year of apprenticeship and their monthly expenses were USD 1,500, their DTI (debt to income) ratio would be at a 28% mark which is considered a manageable level.

If an apprentice made USD 85,000 in their third year of apprenticeship and their monthly expenses were USD

2,500 monthly, their DTI (debt to income) ratio would be at a 35% mark.

As you can see from the numbers, if you're just getting started as an apprentice, you may need to hold off a year or two before making big life-changing purchases. The purpose of showing you these numbers is you want your income to out-pace your debt year over year.

That is a critical element of also reaching your financial freedom goal. I'm not saying debt is wrong; we all need debt to prove we can manage our finances, but the key is managing that debt. For example, make the payments if you buy a new car with a loan. It's simple.

If you buy a new house, make the payments. Again, simple.

As I stated earlier in this chapter, managing debt gets easier and easier as you move through an apprenticeship, and your yearly income continues to rise when you become credentialed. However, I have seen apprentices lose nearly everything because their bank accounts increase, and for some reason, they think it's wise to spend the money on non-necessity purchases.

I try to maintain as little debt load as possible - even though I'm at the top of my pay scale and don't have to check my bank account. I know every week I'll get paid for my skilled labor, and that's all I need to feel comfortable that I'll never be in a financial crisis because of a decision to spend more than I earn. Do I splurge a little here and there? Sure, everyone does.

I knew many years ago that my financial freedom for myself was never worrying about finances, and I don't. I pay my mortgage and make a vehicle payment or two, and that's about it for my regular debt - which is entirely manageable.

To touch back on what we've discussed in this chapter - when you first start as an apprentice, your income will initially be smaller than a few years later when you have more experience and knowledge. Suppose you are joining an apprenticeship from high school or secondary school. In that case, the impact of a first-year apprentice wage might seem like quite a bump in earnings from some of the jobs you may have been working as a student, and that's proof that an apprenticeship is a financially smart decision, as you'd already be earning more money than you were as a student. The pay only gets better as you move through an apprenticeship program!

If you are an adult considering a career change into an apprenticeship, that's an entirely different self-awareness thought process you would have to work through. I've known many adults who switched from corporate life to a construction apprenticeship. Although they took a significant reduction in pay, their mindset was "it's only temporary" as the years go by quickly, which means if you can figure out how to live with the stepped pay structure of an apprenticeship, the good outweighs the bad as it's only a few years before you'll be in the six-figure range.

I think the "six-figure range" type statements I make are geographically specific to whichever region of the US, Canada, or UK you are in. Many factors make up an economic society, and the economics between the three countries are entirely different, so my statements are made from a symbolic point of view. In any country you reside in, apprenticeship and skilled worker wages are at the higher end of the pay spectrum. You can rest assured of that.

Budgeting and Saving

An attainable budget is one of the first things we discuss in an apprenticeship class setting. No one likes to talk about budgets, as the psychology while talking about that gets into your head, and people feel immediately restricted to spending money only for the needed essentials or limited to not going out and spending their hard-earned pay on whatever the heck you want to. So that's where the problems begin, and it's within the thought process of budgeting.

You will go through a regular series of pay raises as an apprentice. You might get a bump of 10% one year, and the following year might be 15%. In the next year or two, you might be in the 20% range, and sooner or later, you'll be at the top of the pay scale. At this point in their apprenticeship, many have healthy bank accounts and, understandably, may be thinking about all the new things they can afford. I've seen apprentices buy brand-new vehicles while in apprenticeship, even though they have a reliable mode of transportation to get them to work and school. I've seen apprentices buy boats and off-road vehicles that they can only use a few times a year because they don't take much time off from work.

I've explained to apprentices for years that if you keep your wants versus your needs in check, you will do fine managing your soon-to-be high-paying job income, but it does take some work.

These are the first talking points I would always throw out during those classes for discussion:

• How much money should you or will you keep in reserve for an emergency?

• How much of your paycheck are you allocating for your needs, such as food, shelter, vehicle maintenance, and incidentals?

• How much are you saving for your "wants" like a vacation, holiday, or socializing?

You will have to address these questions once you start your apprenticeship, as the day will come when you'll look at your paycheck receipt. You'll be "laughing all the way to the bank," as they say because you've possibly never made this much money at a job before. And that is the trap new apprentices fall into, earning more money than they need to live - so why not spend it?

I then start talking about credit cards and the debt trap many young people can get into with the simplicity of using plastic cards to pay for everything. Need a new set of earbuds to listen to your music on the job? Swipe here, please. Are you looking for a new motorized scooter during the spring and summer? Swipe here, please. Do you want to take your mates out for some drinks and a nice dinner and offer to pay for it all because you've got this fabulous apprentice job that pays you great money? Swipe. Here. Please.

It's a mental trap that even some adults can't seem to shake off. It's so easy to whip out a credit card to pay for things, and I'm certainly guilty of it as I don't usually carry much paper money around with me.

I'm sure you can figure out what happens at the end of the month when all your "swipe here please" transactions get tallied up, and the institution written on your card has pre-paid for your month of spending. You guessed it; at the end of the month, you get a nice multi-page breakdown of all the energy drinks, lattes, and hamburgers you've used the card for that month. Then, of course, the outstanding credit card bill says you can pay the minimum amount due, which sure looks attractive on paper if you only have to pay the minimum amount; that leaves more money in your bank account for next month's lousy spending decisions, right? *Wrong.*

The debt trap gets tighter when you pay just the minimum for any bills you might have. There's a little thing called interest that the credit card companies love to charge, and that's why they offer the option of only paying the minimum amount shown on your credit card statement. The credit card company will help you keep your money in the bank by allowing you to make the minimum payment, and you'll help the credit card company make a profit by paying the interest on the unpaid balance for that month.

Don't fall into the credit card trap during the years of your apprenticeship; it's just way too easy to spend every penny of your pay without even knowing it. Additionally, the end-of-the-month surprise in the form of a credit card bill will not suit your ability to budget and save.

You will always need to keep in the back of your mind that if you are spending less than you earn, you're doing it right. So even if your bank account grows very slowly, it's still moving in the right direction.

Just as an apprenticeship is a learning process, so is managing the money you earn from that apprenticeship. If you were in one of my classes, I would tell you that unless disaster strikes, such as your reliable vehicle breaking down and you must be at work the following day, there is no reason to spend beyond your means.

You have wants, and you have needs. The good money you will be making as you move through the years of your apprenticeship is for your needs (with maybe a very occasional want), and the money you make when you have a credential, license, or journey worker card is for your desires.

Saving For Your Future

We've touched on keeping a budget just a bit, and now we will dive into saving a bit more in detail. First, assume you've set a budget and manage your money reasonably well as an apprentice. Your bank account is growing gradually, and you know you're doing a pretty good job not overspending or having outrageous monthly credit card bills.

Now is the time to start thinking about a plan to save for your future, which means retirement. Whichever type of apprenticeship you enter, between a collective bargaining union apprenticeship or a non-union private company non-collective bargaining apprenticeship, you'll have some choices about your future and retirement a few decades later.

Both types of apprenticeships have some very nice benefits available for when you retire. For example, a union type of apprenticeship has a benefits package called "fringe benefits." These fringe benefits are your contribution to a program that can cover some or all parts of healthcare costs, retirement income known as a pension, and possibly even vacation or holiday pay. The contributions to these funds are made by your employer and, in most circumstances, would never be something you could negotiate for as a payment on your regular pay statement.

In a non-union private company apprenticeship, very similarly structured benefits are available, but these might have a different name. Private companies in the US offer their employees the option to take part in what's known as a 401K plan, which is very similar to a pension plan. You contribute your money at the percentage you choose, and the company might or might not increase that contribution in a "401K match". Private companies offer healthcare options to their employees through a company-sponsored or group-sponsored healthcare program, typically a shared cost between the apprentice and the employer. Private companies may also offer paid time off to take vacations or holidays, and this is usually always structured as a "time served" program, meaning the more years of service given to the company, the more paid vacation time you are allotted.

As an apprentice, you should consider your retirement income when you first start your apprenticeship, as it is never too early to plan for retirement. Understandably you might think I'm crazy, as you might be a young adult about to venture out into the working world in your new role as an apprentice, and you've got years to think about retirement.

That is where we would agree to disagree. However, it's never too early to start planning for retirement.

The UK has similar options to a 401K program for workers at private companies, called the Workforce Pension Scheme. The UK takes great pride in knowing that they are taking care of its aging workforce, and it's the younger workers that primarily feed the funds that pay the retirees their pension when those retirees reach the State Pension Age.

Canada also provides retirement income options to their workforce, but it is structured differently than the US employer-sponsored 401K programs. Canadian citizens can set up and manage their Registered Retirement Savings Plans (RRSPs). Both the US 401K program and the Canadian RRSP program are pre-tax deduction programs that employers must adhere to, as RRSPs in Canada are regulated by the Canadian Revenue Agency.

I would suggest that you start saving early in your apprenticeship, even if it's only fifty dollars a week, as that is a manageable amount of income to put away and get you into the habit of saving for your future beyond what your occupational benefits will be.

I want to close out this topic by showing you how saving money in an account with an average compounding interest rate compounds that interest as the fund grows over time.

The first numbers I calculated were for a very attainable $50 weekly contribution to an interest-bearing savings account. The account would pay interest at the average national rate of .25%, and the interest would compound (stack on top of each other) monthly.

Here's a breakdown of how much you would have in your account after 5-year increments for a total period of 30 years:

<u>After five years:</u>

Total amount saved: $13,000

Interest earned: $80.22

Total account balance: $13,080.22

<u>After ten years:</u>

Total amount saved: $26,000

Interest earned: $324.95

Total account balance: $26,324.95

<u>After fifteen years:</u>

Total amount saved: $39,000

Interest earned: $736.26

Total account balance: $39,736.26

<u>After twenty years:</u>

Total amount saved: $52,000

Interest earned: $1,316.25

Total account balance: $53,316.25

After twenty-five years:

Total amount saved: $65,000

Interest earned: $2067.23

Total account balance: $67,067.23

After thirty years:

Total amount saved: $78,000

Interest earned: $2,990.76

Total account balance: $80,990.76

If you saved $50 weekly for the next 30 years, first from your apprentice pay and then from your skilled worker pay, you'd have a nice cash nest egg in the bank that would be a nice bonus to your pension or 401K retirement income, right?

Now let's look at those numbers if you could save $1000 a month into the same type of account. Just remember, as you move through your apprenticeship and into your career if you budget your wants and needs right - $1000 a month saved into your supplemental self-managed retirement savings account is undoubtedly attainable.

After five years:

Total amount saved: $60,000

Interest earned: $607

Total account balance: $60,607

After ten years:

Total amount saved: $120,000

Interest earned: $1,499.76

Total account balance: $121,499.76

After fifteen years:

Total amount saved: $180,000

Interest earned: $3,398.12

Total account balance: $183,398.12

After twenty years:

Total amount saved: $240,000

Interest earned: $6,074.98

Total account balance: $246,074.98

After twenty-five years:

The total amount saved: $300,000

Interest earned: $9,540.94

Total account balance: $309,450.94

After thirty years:

Total amount saved: $360,000

Interest earned: $13,803.51

Total account balance: $373,803.51

Wow. Could you imagine having an extra $373,000 for yourself as an add-on to the retirement plan you worked for three decades to build up? If you took this nearly 375K of self-managed invested money and piggybacked that on what conceivably could be an employer-matched retirement or pension account worth nearly $600,000 USD over the lifespan of your career, welcome to the millionaires club!

It all comes down to budgeting, saving, and having the self-awareness and diligence to make a plan and stick to it. Of course, your plan doesn't have to include a separate interest-bearing savings account if you're against it, and I completely understand that having the diligence to save $1000 a month isn't for everyone.

If you keep it in the back of your mind that the years of your career will tick by one after another, you will hit the glorious stage of retirement when you don't have to get up for work anymore.

Starting a working career as an apprentice is an excellent way to build wealth. All industries and sectors we've discussed in the US, UK, and Canada need skilled workers to replace workers who also started as apprentices about 30 years ago.

These occupations pay very well, and the work is not going away.

I have yet to meet someone that regretted joining an apprenticeship.

8

IT'S A BRIGHT FUTURE

INDUSTRY GROWTH

As of the end of 2021, the number of registered apprenticeship programs in the US nearly surpassed 27,000. However, there needs to be more relevant data in the United Kingdom stating the number of apprenticeship programs, and the UK Parliament says that the number of individual apprentices working in the UK was nearly 740,000.

Would it surprise you that, as of the end of 2021, more apprentices were working in the UK than in the US?

It's hard to imagine, right? It's true. During the fiscal year-end of 2021, the US Government's Department of Labor released its annual report regarding the state of apprenticeships in the United States. The report stated that during 2021, more than 221,000 thousand men and women had entered an apprenticeship, and the active number of apprentices that year, including the new entrants into a program, was 636,000. That government report clarified that the US had just over 100,000 fewer apprentices in the US than the UK in 2021.

It's hard to imagine, but the US is seemingly supposed to be the leader in designing and developing apprenticeship programs, but are they?

In Canada In 2021, the number of newly registered apprentices was in the low 100,000 range, and the total number of registered apprentices throughout the territories and provinces of Canada was nearly 685,000.

Why does this data matter? Because an apprenticeship is a revolving door of sorts. New apprentices sign up, work jobs, attend school, get credentials, and turn out into the workforce as new skilled labor. The cycle continues year after year and will continue for decades to come.

The US, UK, and Canadian governments are using their respective populations of men and women to feed the apprenticeship systems in each country, and it's a model that has seemed to work for the last century. The unfortunate part of the feeder programs, however, is that the number of people interested in apprenticeships does not seem to grow as fast as the industries and sectors that need men and women are losing them. As a result, the growth and subsequent need for skilled labor to fill the occupations in those industries are growing far quicker than people like you can enter the apprenticeship and turn out as credentialed and skilled workers.

The demand is far greater than the supply.

A recent Forbes article states that multiple industries will see double-digit growth through 2035. These industries have been shorthanded for several years, and with the projected growth - they will be even more challenged to find skilled replacement workers for the aging workforce and retirements. (Stahl, 2022).

The in-demand industries that, most recently within the past five years, feel the strain of an ongoing labor shortage are:

- Personal Care & Services
- Travel & Tourism
- Information Technology
- Healthcare
- Construction

These industries are in no particular order; they all need replacement apprentices.

In Personal Care & Services, some of the occupations that continuously see steady demand but have a supply shortfall are:

- Animal Care and Services
- Childcare & Preschool

- Funeral Direction & Funeral Services

- Home Health & Personal Care Aides

The need for skilled workers was paused in the travel industry during the Coronavirus pandemic. However, the recent pandemic has seemingly all but been forgotten, and life has, for the most part, returned to normal, and people are traveling again as more and more countries have opened their borders to tourism.

Some very popular apprenticeships in the Travel & Tourism industry that need apprentices:

- Airline Customer Service Agent

- Airline Pilot

- Cruise Ship - Cabin Crew

- Cruise Ship - Steward

- Hotel Manager

- Interpreter

- Port Operative

- Tour Manager

- Travel Agency Manager

Information Technology has always been an evolving industry that has to shift on the fly to keep up with the technological advancements that continue to propel the world further into the digital and cyber-space age. Years ago, an IT professional typically monitored an incoming phone line to provide "helpline" services for basic computers that you might not even recognize as technological advancement for its time.

The advancements in computing, memory storage devices for all our data needs, and the billion-dollar-a-year cellular phone markets are advancing rapidly. As a result, more and more occupations within that industry are being created and developed yearly.

The Computing Technology Industry Association (CompTIA) lists the fastest-growing Information Technology occupations that can start from an apprenticeship:

• Tech Support Specialist

• Network Support Specialist

• Cybersecurity Support Specialist

• Data Analyst

There's no question the Information Technology industry will not see a drop in the need for skilled replacement workers in the decades to come. From many Governments of the world forming their cybersecurity divisions and nearly every business that uses some form of computing to manage their data - there is a need for skilled workers that understand the workings of digital cyberspace.

The healthcare industry is also experiencing high volume growth as the aging population in every country is creating a need for caring and skilled healthcare workers. In addition, medical technology advancements require many occupations to develop, build, test, and extrapolate data for those advancements to become available in healthcare. The constant turnover of the healthcare industry's aging workforce means that, similar to the IT industry, the healthcare industry will lose its skilled workforce faster than replacement occupation seekers will be available.

In a previous chapter, I touched on some essential healthcare apprenticeships, and here are a few more that seem to be in heavy demand in recent years:

- Audiologist

- Dietitian

- Medical Coder

- Pharmacy Technician

- Phlebotomist

- Radiation Therapist

- Radiology Technician

With the aging populations of nearly every country globally, seeking an apprenticeship within the healthcare industry surely would not be a wrong decision. Additionally, as long as humans are populating this world, there will need to be educated, skilled, and credentialed professionals to provide care for those who need it.

The pre-Covid 19 pandemic projections for the growth of the construction industry between Canada, the US, and the UK saw the United Kingdom taking the top spot at 14% in 2021. The US and Canada had about the same growth rate of nearly 4.5 percent that same year.

Regardless, the need for skilled and credentialed workers is going strong. As I said earlier, the infrastructure in all three countries is aging just as the human population is aging. Structures like homes, commercial buildings, schools, hospitals, airports, sports centers, and more all have a limited amount of time left before many of these buildings will be in the repair or replace category - and that's where the skilled workers take over.

I will close out this Industry Growth topic by saying any of the five most in-demand industries I told you about above are very well worth your time to research further to see if there's an occupation that fits you.

After you're done reading this book, keep in mind while you are doing your research that there will always be people that:

• Need specialized personal services

• Want to travel

• Will have a computer on their desk or a mini-computer cellular device in their pocket or purse

- Need to see a Doctor for specialized care or will need home healthcare if they cannot make it to a medical center

- Need shelter, a place to conduct business, a school for their education, or a hospital for specialized medical care

The five points I made above are a clear example that if you join an apprenticeship in any of the five industries in dire need of a replacement workforce, the projected growth ensures that you can quickly develop a lifelong career and ride that growth through to retirement.

The Labor Shortage

A study was completed 2022 on bringing the labor mismatch in the US construction industry back into line.

McKinsey & Company states that the passage of a US Bipartisan Infrastructure Law will bring a 10-year 550 billion dollar investment into the commercial construction industry. That dollar value represents approximately 3.2 million new jobs within construction over the next decade.

That figure indicates that around 320,000 new construction jobs - union and non-union; will be up for grabs in the next ten years.

The labor shortage still has a huge problem, however, as the last reported data of the shortfall in filling those construction jobs was a deficit of over 400,000 unfilled skilled workforce jobs as of late 2021. The shortfall of skilled workers also creates a practical but exciting problem - depending on which side of the paycheck you are on.

The need for more skilled or credentialed workers to close that 400,000 gap means that labor is in high demand. When skilled labor is in such tall order that it typically triggers revisiting the skilled labor pay structures, a shortage of a skilled labor workforce means that industries and sectors must realize that to attract new replacements for those occupations, the yearly income must be adjusted for those occupations to fall more in line with the economies of each respective country. Economics, such as interest rates and the cost of living, is a significant factor in typical pay within an industry to attract new apprentices. The more substantial demand for a replacement workforce means a higher monetary demand from that workforce which then trickles up to the employers within that industry and sector.

Additional growth from other industries besides construction also affects skilled workers' wages. If construction wages are up, skilled workers in other in-demand workforces also want to reap that better pay scale, so they start working towards a better pay scale or salary.

The IT (information technology) industry nearly mirrors that of construction. Yet, according to some experts, this industry has been hit especially hard with a labor shortage as information technology advances so rapidly that apprenticeship programs in the IT world often need help to keep up with the rapid changes required.

The demand for IT services and technological migration of private company data during the Covid-19 pandemic was astounding, and the IT industry was surprised at the sheer number of companies that at the start of the pandemic needed to make a data switch - and very rapidly. Companies must support the new working-from-home model brought on by the pandemic to maintain some normalcy in their revenues. IT companies came to the rescue, and that's when their industry proved to be so understaffed.

The amount of occupational training (also known as apprenticeship) has increased five-fold since the start of the pandemic. With nearly all Covid-19 protocols lifting from 2022 to early 2023, the immediate need for IT on demand and in a hurry has lessened. Still, it was a wake-up call to the IT industry that the demand outweighs the supply, and the industry is heavily recruiting for the future of IT and Cyber Security for the next decade.

As I said, much like construction, the technology industry is also a sure bet that you can find an apprenticeship that will suit your interests. Understandably, only some people like getting up at the crack of dawn to meet the sunrise and start their workday as most construction professionals do, so another viable option for a growing and in-demand industry is the technology industry with a career path in IT if you prefer working during regular business hours.

Just as there will always be construction projects rebuilding the aging infrastructure in many countries, healthcare will remain an in-demand industry as populations age, and so will the information technology industry be constantly evolving as more cyberspace landscape appears.

There isn't a lot of factual data regarding labor shortages in the UK, and plausibly because the UK far surpasses the US and Canada by the number of individual apprentices in the workforce.

There is a website called davidsonmorris.com in the UK that explains the UK Shortage Occupation List tied to apprenticeships, so if you are a UK reader of this book - you should check out that website. The list details the occupation codes for each listed occupation, explains the type of job and areas of the UK affected by the shortage, and the annual salary is displayed with an adjustment for an apprentice wage in that same occupation code. (Morris, 2023).

The volume of information pointing towards the nearly global shortage of skilled workers to fill the occupations being vacated by the older generations is daunting. I researched many well-known labor industry websites with years and years' worth of labor data that I could have passed along to you within this book, but I couldn't justify creating many more chapters to present the expert studies and the results of those studies.

The US, Uk, and Canada have all had industrial revolutions of nearly immeasurable size, and those advancements centuries ago led to the "blue collar" moniker that describes the skilled craftspeople that emerged in those years. However, advances in technology have indeed modernized many of the processes within the most affected industries with labor shortages, and there is a large percentage of those occupations that will never be clear of the need for professionally skilled individuals to further the building and rebuilding of the infrastructure that first appeared in earlier centuries.

The need for skilled labor within the in-demand industries is constant, and that opens the door for anyone like yourself to seek an apprenticeship while learning lifelong skills that will provide a healthy yearly income and benefits to sustain you through your retirement years.

I have seen the need for apprentices firsthand within multiple industries for many decades, and that need is sustainable for many decades to come.

SUCCESSFUL PATHS THROUGH APPRENTICESHIP

Jacob, Cam, and Kelly

Throughout this book, I've been telling you that I've spent many years in an apprenticeship training program educational facility working as an instructor. I've also said to you that I thoroughly love doing so.

I love seeing the excitement and wonderment of the apprentices as they arrive for their first full day of classes, just as much as I love attending a graduation dinner where they're sent off into the working world as new credentialed and licensed journey workers.

The hours spent between their first day and their last day in the apprenticeship program are my research. On those days, I can pull a young man or young lady aside and ask,

"Do you mind if I ask......" and then whichever bit of information I'm looking for might be answered.

Only some people want to tell their story. For those that do, I ask them if they mind if I take a few notes and most graciously approve. I'll tell you about three people whose stories have stood out to me as they relate to the self-awareness we've talked about in addition to career development which is entirely up to every individual worker. Whether someone works in an apprenticeship and becomes a credentialed skilled worker or not, everyone in the working world can take their career in any direction they choose.

I've included my recollections of three amiable people willing to share their apprenticeship and career development stories with me and why they chose an apprenticeship career path instead of the expensive college path.

JACOB

Jacob was forty-two years old when he realized he wasn't happy with his US Government job working as a data analyst anymore. The day I talked to Jacob was his 46th birthday, and he was a fourth-year apprentice working in the construction industry. I hadn't known Jacob before this day, as the class I was teaching was missing an instructor that evening, and I was asked to step in.

I heard one of the other apprentices give this fellow a birthday greeting, so I thought I might as well too. When I asked Jacob how old he had turned on the day of our class, he commented it was his 46th birthday, and I immediately when into inquisitive mode.

Forty-six is slightly different from a typical apprentice age, at least not in the construction industry. Construction provides many opportunities to push your body to the limit, constantly use your muscle groups in your daily tasks, and sometimes work in extreme heat or cold, depending on a geographical area. Although a person who enters the construction industry as an older individual can learn the trade, perform the work, and be very successful, the typical demographic for entry-level construction positions is individuals aged 18 to 28.

I had congratulated Jacob on turning 46 and then had asked him if he'd tell me how he came to the apprenticeship and what his motives were.

Jacob had told me about the "good" job he left with the US Government. He had attended a four-year bachelor's degree program some 20-plus years before and, luckily, had paid off his $48,000 in student loan debt within ten years after his college commencement. After that, he settled into his career, and Jacob told me he was pretty good at it. He had received numerous accolades within his department in his years of service, and being that he was working for the US Government, he had amassed an impressive paid time off schedule and quite a bit of pension credit.

At that point in his story, I stopped him mid-sentence of what he was about to say and asked, "Why"? Why would you leave a job where you could take 2.5 months of work off each year and get paid for it? Why would you leave a position where you have a Government pension? (In full transparency - I have never looked at data to understand what the US Government pays their pensioners).

Jacob responded to my questions, "I just wasn't happy." I get that, but I'd need him to expand on that.

Jacob told me he'd been sitting in the same office, in the same building, with the same window view for 22 years. Every day he went to his office, hung up his coat, and would head to the office lunch room, and put his lunch in the refrigerator. Then, on the way back to his office, he would stop and grab his coffee cup out of the cup holder, fill it, and then walk back into his office to start his day.

He'd turn on his computer and spend the next eight hours crunching numbers and collecting data. He also told me he would take two government-mandated daily breaks and crunch numbers between those breaks.

When Jacob explained his day-in and day-out working life, it was much more colorful than how I explained it to you. When he told me about his previous career, I almost felt like I was listening to a narrated version of many movies we might watch where the office professional is stuck in a rut. Every workday feels like it's on a continual loop of the same thing day after day.

After Jacob finished his version of why he left his job and what he "just couldn't do anymore," I asked how he arrived at construction as his next career venture.

Jacob told me that he had been happily married for several years and had a child, and one thing he enjoyed doing with his child was building things (on a small scale level). Jacob and his child had built birdhouses, a small skateboard ramp for the child, and a cutting board or two that was nicely varnished that Jacob's child had given the mother as a gift.

Jacob also told me that he regularly dreamt about just about every other occupation he could get into that might bring him some career satisfaction. Unfortunately, Jacob came up short in just about every thought he had. He had thought about what else he could do with his life that wouldn't disrupt his family unit and wouldn't mean going back to an expensive college to get an additional degree if that needed to be done.

Jacob had told me that just as often as he would dream about being able to carve out a new career, he also would dream about this next woodworking project he and his child could do. Through the self-awareness of his situation, Jacob realized the answer was right in front of him, but he hadn't identified it as clearly as when he was thinking hard about what a career change looked like for him.

Jacob's greatest joys, he said, were working with his child in his homemade makeshift wood shop, sawing, hammering, and nailing things together to produce a tangible item. Something he could stand back and say to his child, "Look at that, we built that."

Jacob eventually knew he'd be shifting careers; he just didn't know how to get there. So he called a few of the local builder's organizations and got as much information as possible about becoming a carpenter. Jacob loved the smell of wood, so it seemed natural to him.

He secured an apprenticeship with a contractor in his area, and that contractor took him on as an apprentice. They offered him great starting pay and excellent benefits. In addition, they allowed Jacob to go through a builders organization apprenticeship school two evenings a week during the school year for three years.

At the end of the three-year apprenticeship, Jacob was credentialed and certified through the builder's organization and received full journey worker pay. Jacob then commented that although a mid-life career shift was frightening, he knew that the end result of his three-year apprenticeship was well worth the sacrifice of not having the steady income he had as a US Government employee. It was only three years before he'd be financially back to where he was when he left his job.

Jacob's story is a very unique story based on his age. Jacob is possibly in the last 15 years of his career, and his initial decision to seek an apprenticeship was difficult for him. However, when Jacob finally understood his self-awareness that his happiness lay in the tools he used and the satisfaction from building those things, he knew what sort of apprenticeship he sought.

CAMERON

I met Cam when he started in the apprenticeship where I regularly teach. Cam was very quiet when he first came to my class, and it almost seemed that Cam was shy or reserved as he didn't interact much with the other dozen apprentices.

When class was dismissed on our second evening, I checked in with Cam to ensure he was ok, and he assured me he was. Cam had said this was such a new environment for him that he didn't want to miss any information I was discussing as it may be necessary. It was then I realized that Cam was super nervous about being in an adult learning environment, as Cam was surrounded by early to mid-twenty-somethings who all had come to an apprenticeship after realizing that college was not the path for them.

Cam was nineteen when he started in my class, and because he was so young, I talked with him after class one evening and asked if he'd share his story about how he landed in an apprenticeship.

Cam told me he had an older sibling off at a private college. So Cam's final two years of high school were spent listening to his parents have discussions with his older sibling about the cost of college, the need for student loans for Cam's sibling, and just the general conversations that were had about the college experience and the dollar figures that go along with a four-year college degree.

Cam explained that he had started working at a fast-food restaurant job when he turned fifteen years old and was very good at saving money. Cam told me he'd amassed a nice bit of money in the bank, and the discussions at home about his older sibling going to college were very troubling for Cam as he realized he didn't see the point of college when he could work and earn money.

Cam's parents explained that he needed a career, and the only way to get that career was through the military or college. So when the time came closer to his high school graduation, Cam and his parents would figure out how much in college loans Cam would need to get because his parents couldn't help with the college cost.

Cam said he had researched alternatives to college for the next year or so while telling his parents he was researching college. Finally, Cam saw an ad on a social media site promoting construction and the building trades and had a link to click to see a day in the life of an apprentice. Cam said he clicked the link, and after watching the three-minute video, he knew what he would do with his life after high school.

Cam contacted the organization that made the video that he clicked on, and the organization gave Cam the full details on where, when, and how to apply for the apprenticeship Cam was seeking acceptance to.

The application period coincided with his high school commencement date, so Cam immediately applied for the apprenticeship right after high school. He also told me the application process and the interview were relatively easy for him, and the required aptitude test that checked for basic math, English, and reading skills was a breeze.

Cam's story is typical: if you want something, go after it. Cam was not going to follow in his older siblings' footsteps of going to an expensive private college and having to take student loans to do so. Instead, he told me with much confidence in his voice that he knew there was another way to find a career he could be proud of, and he just happened to see a social media post that pointed him in the right direction.

Cam entered a five-year stepped-pay collective bargaining apprenticeship and has on-the-job training every day as he's given tasks to do and has guidance and oversight by the journey worker trainers. Cam started his apprenticeship at a bit less than half of what those journey workers get paid, and as Cam moves through the years of his apprenticeship, his pay will grow by about 10-15% each year.

When Cam finishes his apprenticeship, Cam will become a credentialed skilled tradesperson and will be another success story that started as an apprentice.

If you're wondering what happened to Cam's older sibling as I was when Cam finished telling me his apprenticeship story, Cam let me know that his sibling struggled a bit at the first private college the sibling attended. Then the sibling transferred to a private college closer to Cam's hometown, and the sibling also struggled there before deciding to leave college altogether and make a new plan.

Cam's older sibling ended up joining the US military and is using the military as a path to a career in a highly specialized occupation in the Information Technology industry. Cam's older sibling left college with a few hefty student loans and will be paying off those loans for many years.

KELLY

Kelly is a gal that also is an apprenticeship instructor in our local area. It was appropriate to include her story as she has a very successful career that started from an apprenticeship, and I asked Kelly if I could share her story in my book. She agreed but on the condition that I don't use her real name, but I assure you the account of her story is accurate.

I don't know much of Kelly's back story about how she became a skilled trades apprentice, but I do know that she didn't go to college. She worked for a few years after high school to find something she liked to do, but nothing ever fit well for her. Kelly had a relative working as a linesman in the industrial energy sector, and he suggested she try a skilled trade apprenticeship.

Kelly told her relative that she was very wary that it wouldn't be a good fit as, in her words, "women don't get treated very well in a man's world." However, her relative quickly let her know that women in the construction industry are respected just as men are, so that theory was put to rest immediately.

Kelly found an apprenticeship in a collective bargaining piping trades union and spent her five years of training learning as much as possible. Kelly told me that as an apprentice, she always had felt like an equal while working alongside men, and quite often would get partnered up with a male apprentice to complete their daily tasks on the job site.

Kelly said she had learned quickly that her misconception about gender inequality was true and that everyone working in construction and industrial energy was there to work together and get the job done.

Kelly completed her apprenticeship and continued in the trade for several years. Then she decided she wanted to try the "business" side of the construction industry. Kelly became a project manager responsible for large and small projects, some with project costs in the millions of dollars.

Kelly excelled as a project manager for many years and then had the opportunity to work at the State government level within the Department of Labor office, overseeing state-funded construction projects. Kelly is only a few years away from retirement when this book is published, and I'm pretty sure she will retire from her position with the state as a very proud woman working within the construction industry.

Kelly had the drive right from the start of her apprenticeship to succeed, coming in with a preconceived notion about gender inequality in the construction industry first and in the skilled trades second. Nevertheless, Kelly took the necessary steps in her career development to mold and shape a path for herself that allowed her to completely control her career and create unique opportunities along the way that, although they were still in the industry, were just different occupations.

The three stories I've told you are similar, yet the people differ. Jacob and Cam had already made decisions to research and enter an apprenticeship, where Kelly just took a suggestion from a relative, and that suggestion provided Kelly with a long and sustainable career.

All three people told me they wouldn't have changed their decision.

I don't always get apprentices to open up to me about why or how they chose an apprenticeship, and that is understandable, as some people are just private people.

I also ask apprentices random questions now and then, such as "Can you give me three reasons why you chose an apprenticeship or why you would suggest an apprenticeship to a friend or even a stranger you've met on the street?". A few of the responses to those questions are below:

- I wasn't an outstanding student and knew I could get into an apprenticeship with just my GED (General Education Diploma).

- I travel around during the day in my service truck; I'm not stuck on a job for 8 hours a day.

- I couldn't get the benefits and pay to work in a bank.

- It's a very mentally rewarding career. Every day I stand back and look at what I've built.

- It's a great starting point because someday I want to own a construction business.

- I wouldn't have been able to find another job that teaches me what I need to know to be successful and also pays me to learn on the job.

- I didn't take my SATs or ACTs in high school, so I didn't think a college would take me. But it all worked out because those college entrance tests aren't required for an apprenticeship.

- Apprenticeship is a legitimate career path that fully trains me to do everything for my job.

- College wasn't for me, and I wouldn't waste money and get myself into debt trying to make everyone happy.

- The low cost of education is a significant return on my investment of a few years in an apprenticeship.

- The hours I work are great, and I don't have to work weekends. A lot of regular business people work weekends.

- The construction industry never slows; they always build things and need skilled trades.

- I'll never have to live paycheck to paycheck again.

There you have it. Many of the responses to the quick random questions I ask when I've got my instructor hat on.

GRATIFICATION FROM A GOOD DAY'S WORK

There is one response I seem to get over and over again, even now, when I ask the same questions I started asking around a decade ago.

The response has to do with the answer above about the construction industry being a very mentally rewarding career. Every trade can be mentally satisfying as you get out of a job what you put into it. However, my belief is a bit subjective, as I know some people work in fields they're not happy with or feel stuck in a career with no upward trajectory of advancement into other aspects of the job - like Kelly's story.

Going back over the years of notes I've taken about the people whom I've asked to share their stories with me, the most frequent response I've gotten was somehow related to the benefit of being able to stand back and look at what that person has either installed, built or designed - which leads to the mental stimulation comments. People who use their minds to create things with their hands appreciate the ability to do so, and that's why I've rarely found a disgruntled or adverse person in the industry.

Reviewing those notes, I realized I've never researched the correlation between hands-on jobs and mentally rewarding occupations. So I was pretty surprised by some of the data I found.

Interestingly enough, on the North Bennet Street School website, I found a news story explaining some well-stated theories on the benefits of working with your hands and how that affects one's personality. The North Bennet St. School is located in Boston, Massachusetts; this vocational school has for nearly 150 years been providing hands-on vocational training and community outreach, initially to Irish immigrants and now to anyone that wishes to attend.

The article on the North Bennet St. School site explains that we alter our brain chemistry simply by working with our hands. The report says that the benefits of working with your hands create a form of inner peace just as much as it promotes mindfulness and reduces anxiety. Managing stress and enhancing concentration and sleep patterns are also mentioned as benefits of a hands-on career.

The unknown author of the article continues by commenting that the modern-day younger generation(s) are conflicted with the thought of entering a four-year college program that likely will result in an income bracket that doesn't seem commensurate with the high cost of college and that the younger generation now is trending towards apprenticeships as the "alternative college degree" that pays well right from the start.

Additionally, the article concludes with the thought process that the stigma surrounding skilled trades careers is due to the devaluation of skilled and manual labor as a necessary and beneficial career option required to rebuild our aging infrastructure. The final thought of the article states that humans are wired for creativity, and it's through that creativity and working with your hands that provides gratification and personal accomplishment while working in a hands-on career field.

I couldn't have explained it better myself - even though I've been working in a hands-on field for over 25 years and know firsthand how fulfilling it is to stand back at the end of the day and look at what I've created from parts and pieces.

10

FINAL THOUGHTS

MY HUMBLE APPRECIATION

I hope you understand everything as I've presented it in this book. I'm sure by now you've figured out you'll probably want to do some research about apprenticeships to follow up your reading of this book. If there's one thing I can suggest over all others – it's never to count out an apprenticeship because you know nothing about an industry, occupation, or what the apprenticeship model looks like for that career path.

Because you've read this far, I'm assuming you have a much better understanding of how an apprenticeship is a way to a lifelong career in an under-served and in-demand industry. In an apprenticeship, you'll receive great pay during your on-the-job training years, and after your apprenticeship, you will have a life-long skillset that you didn't have when you entered the apprenticeship; and if you stick with it through your entire career; you will have a very nice retirement income.

I've been as upfront and honest with you as possible about what to expect in your apprenticeship search and have tried to remember to include every little detail that may affect your decision-making process - whether the details were related to working hours, job conditions, pay, benefits, or any host of other things I've talked about in this book.

I've given you data on multiple industries and sectors in danger of being unable to fill the voids left by an aging workforce. If those industries cannot sustain the work due to a lack of interested apprentices, they might find alternative ways of conducting their business instead of using skilled human labor.

I've told you a few success stories of apprentices who figured things out on their own, and I've told you about my own experience of how I ended up in an apprenticeship that I had no intention of joining until I was out of options but appreciated the opportunity right from the start.

The US, UK, and Canada (along with the rest of the countries of the world), at some point in their development centuries ago, were built using some form of apprenticeship, although under conditions that did not favor the worker. Nevertheless, apprenticeships are an excellent program for all involved parties, and it doesn't matter the industry.

The biggest thing I want you to consider about an apprenticeship is that it's your ticket to a nearly debt-free start to your life in the working world. The majority of your peers are all thinking about college. Unfortunately, I'm guessing that most of them might be unable to write a check for every penny of that education. There's only one option if that's the case - and the option is the "for profit" college loan lenders that don't care if someone is having a hard time in college and needs to take a break.

Those college lenders also don't care that you might have to take a temporary leave from college because a relative is sick. Those lenders don't care when you started college or why you decided to leave college. They don't care that as a new college graduate, you're having a hard time finding a job because you're competing with millions of same-age people as yourself who all want the same thing you do - and that's to get a great job with benefits that you can make a lifelong career from.

The college loan lenders only care for you to return the money they gave you, the profit they will make off the money they lent to you in the form of interest, and fees they might charge for late payments if that should ever happen.

The last thing I will share with you regarding the college conversation is how that affects young adults like you and how incredibly expensive it is to repay college loans. I genuinely wish there were zillions of hours of skilled work to perform every year, and young adults would no longer feel pressured to go to college to fulfill the college agenda set decades ago.

The National Association of Scholars reported on the bullet points below in February 2021. The article was titled "Priced Out: What college costs America." (Arnold, 2021).

- As of 2018, 44 Million Americans owe more than 1.5 trillion dollars in student debt.

- In 1980, the average cost for a four-year public university degree was $5,100.

- In 2019, the same four-year degree came with a price tag of over $25,000. A 4-year private college tuition room and board in 2018 was nearing $39,000.

- New, first-time college students in 2018 will have graduated with an average student loan debt of $35,000. In addition, most graduates will need 20 years to repay their student loans.

Those four bullet points above have hopefully sealed your decision to seek an apprenticeship. Suppose you find an apprenticeship, complete the schooling, and have completed your apprenticeship term. I will all but guarantee you that you will never resemble even one single statistic I've listed in this book - other than maybe a brand new statistic of masses of young people that refuse to feed the collegiate debt cycle and are deciding to let someone pay them to learn a career instead of going into debt.

Finally, these are the main benefits of joining an apprenticeship which I hope will stay fresh in your mind as you continue to research an apprenticeship that will be a good fit for you.

- **You get paid to build your career.** This seems like a "too good to be true" statement, and it's entirely true, I assure you. You will be paid from day one of your apprenticeship and on-the-job training. You will get regular advancements in pay as you progress through an apprenticeship program, and you will be paid regularly. Depending on the apprenticeship industry, you will get paid every week or bi-monthly.

- **You receive a very affordable education.** You will be required to attend apprenticeship classes for the designated amount of required classroom hours, and these classes are designed specifically for the occupation of your apprenticeship. In addition, you may be required to pay a portion of the education cost. A typical apprentice contribution to their yearly education cost ranges from USD 300 to USD 1000 for each year of their apprenticeship. (All apprenticeships have different education costs, and you should familiarize yourself with your selected apprenticeship education program).

- **You are all but guaranteed work for decades.** The labor shortages in each of the industries are not a farce. Experts have tracked these industries for decades and made regular projections about the outlook. Everything I've told you in the book points towards "a workforce marketplace," which is an excellent way of saying the workforce has the advantage due to business booming in the industries, and the employers in those industries are screaming for replacement workers.

- **You will avoid years, possibly decades, of student loan debt.** This statement isn't for everybody; I understand that. There might be some people that can write a check for four years of school. If that is the case - I commend you on your ability to write a four year tuition check in one fell swoop, and unfortunately, you are not the target reader of this book, but I appreciate you reading it this far. I've made it very clear in the book that if you are even giving the cost of college just a slight pause, this book is for you.

- **By entering the workforce with ZERO student loan debt.** This factor is arguably the one that brings you the most significant ability to start building wealth. Getting a jump on your retirement income planning will become very attainable in your apprenticeship.

Additionally, you will be well ahead of your peers when they're done with college as you will already be financially stable and working within your career and earn your living weekly or bi-weekly. *I attach a caveat star to this bullet point as it goes without saying that I do not have data on every single apprenticeship available in the US, UK, or Canada. That means that although there's no guarantee that an individual will not need to borrow money to pay for the required schooling of an apprenticeship, the apprenticeship model of training is an earn-while-you-learn model, and education costs are at a minimum.

As I've stated in previous chapters, the typical apprenticeship education investment covers basic supplies, possibly a technology fee, and some incidentals. I've known students who've paid a few hundred dollars. I've also known students who have paid up to five or six hundred dollars each year of their multi-year apprenticeship. These fees were typical to cover the cost of a laptop or similar device required in a technology-driven apprenticeship. Simply stated, the monetary cost of an apprenticeship education dwarfs the cost of a traditional college by tens of thousands of dollars each year.

Please listen to me when I tell you this: I was a high school dropout who also dropped out of two colleges, leaving me with debt that I couldn't repay until years later. I happened upon an apprenticeship, and I did what I needed to do to be successful in that apprenticeship and out on the job. I always considered my occupation a career, not just a job, as I always pushed myself to improve. I've had hard days at work and some glorious days as well.

I have been financially secure for the better part of the last 25 years, as I've always known that as long as I continue to bring value to my employer, I will have a career to get me through to retirement. I will also retire financially secure, as that's the "end game" of sorts in a skilled labor career. We work to get the paycheck that covers what we need to live on while we are in our working years, and we also work to build up our retirement funds to provide income when we reach our retirement years.

Anyone, and I mean anyone, can find an industry and an occupation in which they would like to enter an apprenticeship. Apprenticeships are open to everyone, and that's all there is to it. There's no monetary deposit for an apprenticeship, no "90-day probation period", and no "we will just try you out for a few days and see how you work out." If you get accepted into an apprenticeship, that's it – you are in.

If you want to be in an apprenticeship - it's yours to lose. What that means is, if you want it - there's only yourself in the way if you don't get the apprenticeship. Apprenticeships are considered a job interview, except the interviews are a bit more detailed as this is an interview for a decades-long career - meaning they don't just hand out apprenticeships that literally could change the course of the recipients' life. Nevertheless, apprenticeships are a coveted opportunity, and I'm 100% certain you have what it takes to get accepted into your program. I know this because I've given you everything you need to know about apprenticeships, and I've told you everything I know about how to find an apprenticeship, apply, interviewing, and following up after an interview, and how to manage your career and finances as you build your career.

My career story could easily be swapped with anyone else's, which means my story is just not that extraordinary; it's the opposite. I'm not unique, and I'm very aware of that. I am, however, a pretty average guy who is still determined to keep pushing myself to succeed after making one wrong decision after another as a young man before I was given the opportunity of an apprenticeship, thanks to my Dad. Quite possibly, what has driven me to have as successful of a career in construction as possible; likely was the fact that I've never received a high school diploma (I did receive my GED the summer after I quit high school), and I've never walked across a stage and flipped that crazy-colored tassel to the other side of a graduation hat.

We all have a driving force within us, and some folks call that grit. My grit still pushes me to succeed a quarter century after I started my career from an apprenticeship. That grit will hopefully see me walk a community college stage in the next few years as I accept an Applied Science degree in a program related to teaching adult learners, which is exactly what an apprenticeship is – an adult learning environment where everyone starts the same on day one, as an apprentice in a new career. You'll have good and bad days in your apprenticeship; that's just the nature of being a human in the adult working world. You'll need to find and keep hold of your grit, as there's a proverbial rainbow at the end of your apprenticeship. That rainbow is a well-deserved yearly income with fantastic benefits that will provide you with the lifestyle and financial success that many people your age don't know is available for just a small fraction of the cost of a traditional college program.

It will be a new and exciting time in your life, and the sky is the limit on how far YOU choose to take your career.

I wish you much success in your journey toward apprenticeship. I know you will be successful while in your training and when you transition from apprenticeship into the working world.

Just by reading this book to the end, you have a level up on your peers. Quite likely, some of those peers may already have anxiety about entering a four-year college program, its associated costs, and the challenge of trying to start their lives in debt that could have been avoided.

I sincerely thank you for reading this book, and I look forward to someday hearing the success story of your apprenticeship.

P.D. Mason

Spread the Word!

There's an exciting road ahead of you, and you're just at the start of it. This is your chance to help someone else discover their career success through the path of Apprenticeship.

Simply by sharing your honest opinion of this book and a little about what you found here, you'll help other young people find the essential guidance they'll never get in high school.

Thank you so much for your support. Your role is vital, and I appreciate you tremendously.

Scan the QR code to leave your review on Amazon.

ABOUT THE AUTHOR

Paul "P.D." Mason lives in the upper Midwest region of the United States with his wife and his trusted writing companion, a knee-high pit bull terrier mix named Sugar. Paul is an independent author writing for SugarDog Publishing and has written multiple fiction and non-fiction books on various topics and fictional storylines that resonate with his readers.

ALSO BY P.D. MASON

Financially Smart Career Planning For Teens: The Roadmap to Making Informed Decisions In An Uncertain Job Market, Prevent Feeling Overwhelmed & Analysis Paralysis To Achieve Affordable College Degrees (2023, SugarDog Publishing)

Skilled Trade Career Planning For Teens: The Handbook of Lucrative Skilled Trades & High Paying Occupations That Don't Require Expensive College Degrees (2023, SugarDog Publishing)

Travel Japan: Unveiling Culture, Language & Local Gems (2023, SugarDog Publishing)

8 Simple Techniques For Easy Kitchen Knife Sharpening: Keep Your Home Kitchen Knives Sharp Using Trusted Tools, Methods & Techniques Taught By Professionals! (2023, SugarDog Publishing)

REFERENCES

"6 Skills & Traits Each Apprentice Should Have to Succeed." *Notgoingtouni*, 22 Jan. 2021, www.notgoingtouni.co.uk/blog/6-skills-traits-each-apprentice-should-have-succeed. Accessed 23 Apr. 2023.

"17 Remarkable Career Change Statistics to Know (2021)." *Apollo Technical LLC*, 25 June 2021, www.apollotechnical.com/career-change-statistics/. Accessed 6 May 2023.

"America Was Built by the Hands of Apprentices." *Blog.michiganconstruction.com*, 14 Nov. 2017, blog.michiganconstruction.com/national-apprenticeship-week-the-history-of-apprenticeships-in-america-0. Accessed 21 Apr. 2023.

"Apprenticeship by Industry Sector." *The Apprenticeship Guide*, apprenticeshipguide.co.uk/apprenticeship-category/industry-sectors/. Accessed 22 Apr. 2023.

Apprenticeship, Office of. "Apprenticeship Industries." *Apprenticeship.gov*, www.apprenticeship.gov/apprenticeship-industries. Accessed 22 Apr. 2023.

---. "Our History." *Apprenticeship.gov*, www.apprenticeship.gov/about-us/our-history. Accessed 20 Apr. 2023.

Apprenticeship: Earn While You Learn.

"Apprenticeships for Tech | CompTIA." *Default*, www.comptia.org/content/lp/apprenticeships-for-tech. Accessed 29 Apr. 2023.

Aspiration. "Top 10 Reasons to Do an Apprenticeship." *Aspiration Training*, 18 Mar. 2019, www.aspirationtraining.com/top-10-reasons-to-do-an-apprenticeship/. Accessed 23 Apr. 2023.

"Become an Apprentice." *GOV.UK*, www.gov.uk/become-apprentice. Accessed 25 Apr. 2023.

Bouchrika, Imed. "Percentage of High School Graduates That Go to College in the U.S. By State & Demographics." *Research.com*, 23 May 2022, research.com/education/percentage-of-high-school-graduates-that-go-to-college.

Bryant, Jessica. "College Dropout Rate in the U.S. | BestColleges." *Www.bestcolleges.com*, 6 Sept. 2022, www.bestcolleges.com/research/college-dropout-rate/#:~:text=Data%20Summary. Accessed 19 Apr. 2023.

c) Copyright skillsyouneed.com 2011-2019. "University vs Apprenticeships | SkillsYouNeed." *Skillsyouneed.com*, 2011, www.skillsyouneed.com/rhubarb/university-vs-apprenticeship.html. Accessed 21 Apr. 2023.

Canada, Employment and Social Development. "Provincial and Territorial Apprenticeship Programs." *Www.canada.ca*, 16 Dec. 2014, www.canada.ca/en/services/jobs/training/support-skilled-trades-apprentices/provinces-territories.html. Accessed 24 Apr. 2023.

Canada, Service. "Supports for Skilled Trades and Apprenticeship." *Www.canada.ca*, 25 July 2018, www.canada.ca/en/services/jobs/training/support-skilled-trades-apprentices.html.

"Career Paths." *United Association*, ua.org/join-the-ua/career-paths/. Accessed 27 Apr. 2023.

Christensen, Todd. "What Is Financial Freedom?" *Https://Www.moneyfit.org/*, 28 Feb. 2022, www.moneyfit.org/financial-freedom-means/.

"College Dropout Rates [2022] - US Statistics and Data." *Think Impact*, 5 Mar. 2021, www.thinkimpact.com/college-dropout-rates/#:~:text=40%25%20of%20students%20drop%20out. Accessed 25 Apr. 2023.

Coursera. "What Are Professional Development Goals? 10 Examples and How to Set Them." *Coursera*, 28 Feb. 2023, www.coursera.org/articles/professional-development-goals. Accessed 28 Apr. 2023.

Duffin, Erin. "U.S. College Enrollment Statistics 1965-2027 | Statista." *Statista*, Statista, 13 Mar. 2020, www.statista.com/statistics/183995/us-college-enrollment-and-projections-in-public-and-private-institutions/. Accessed 24 Apr. 2023.

"Earn & Learn through Apprenticeships." *Career Vision*, careervision.org/earn-learn-through-apprenticeships/. Accessed 26 Apr. 2023.

"Glossary of Apprenticeship Terms | Mass.gov." *Www.mass.gov*, 15 Feb. 2023, www.mass.gov/info-details/glossary-of-apprenticeship-terms#a-e-. Accessed 21 Apr. 2023.

Government of Canada, Statistics Canada. "The Daily — Registered Apprenticeship Training Programs, 2021." *Www150.Statcan.gc.ca*, 6

Dec. 2022, www150.statcan.gc.ca/n1/daily-quotidien/221206/dq221206d-eng.htm. Accessed 24 Apr. 2023.

Hovnanian, Garo , et al. "Solving US Construction's Worker Shortage | McKinsey." *Www.mckinsey.com*, 28 Mar. 2022, www.mckinsey.com/capabilities/operations/our-insights/bridging-the-labor-mismatch-in-us-construction.

"How to Prepare for an Apprenticeship Interview." *UCAS*, 3 Dec. 2019, www.ucas.com/apprenticeships/how-apply-apprenticeship/how-prepare-apprenticeship-interview. Accessed 27 Apr. 2023.

Indeed.com. "How to Apply to Apprenticeships in 7 Easy Steps. ." *Indeed*, 30 Sept. 2022, www.indeed.com/career-advice/finding-a-job/how-to-apply-for-apprenticeships. Accessed 24 Apr. 2023.

Law Donut. "Plumber Legal Issues." *Www.lawdonut.co.uk*, www.lawdonut.co.uk/business/sector-specific-law/plumber-legal-issues#:~:text=What%20licences%20does%20a%20plumber. Accessed 24 Apr. 2023.

"Learn.org -." *Learn.org*, learn.org/articles/How_Long_is_Apprenticeship_Training_Typically.html. Accessed 26 Apr. 2023.

Morris, Anne. "Shortage Occupation List 2021 | DavidsonMorris." *Davidson Morris*, Mar. 2023, www.davidsonmorris.com/shortage-occupation-list/. Accessed 29 Apr. 2023.

Nesbit, Josephine. "The Ultimate Dictionary of Apprenticeship Terms for Employers | Firebrand Learn." *Firebrand.training*, 25 Feb. 2023, firebrand.training/uk/learn/apprenticeships/additional-resources/ultimate-dictionary-of-apprenticeship-terms-for-employers. Accessed 20 Apr. 2023.

"No Experience Apprenticeship: What Is It? And How to Become One?" *ZipRecruiter*, www.ziprecruiter.com/career/No-Experience-Apprenticeship/What-Is-How-to-Become. Accessed 28 Apr. 2023.

North America's Building Trades Unions. *Why a Union Apprenticeship?* Aug. 2021.

Perna, Mark C. "In a Shifting Education Marketplace, the College Degree No Longer Reigns Supreme." *Forbes*, 4 Oct. 2022, www.forbes.com/sites/markcperna/2022/10/04/in-a-shifting-education-marketplace-the-college-degree-no-longer-reigns-supreme/?sh=5fdac1305ad4. Accessed 26 Apr. 2023.

Polzin, Roland. "The Shortage of Tech Workers Can Be Solved by Hiring from This Region." *Entrepreneur*, 8 Mar. 2023, www.entrepreneur.com/growing-a-business/the-shortage-of-tech-workers-can-be-solved-by-hiring-from/446245. Accessed 29 Apr. 2023.

Rutkowski, Barbara. "Benefits of Working with Your Hands, and Why We All Should | NBSS." *North Bennet Street School*, 4 Apr. 2022, nbss.edu/news-events/news-stories/benefits-working-hands-on/. Accessed 30 Apr. 2023.

"Sallie Mae." *Wikipedia*, 16 Jan. 2022, en.wikipedia.org/wiki/Sallie_Mae. Accessed 25 Apr. 2023.

Smith, Heather. "Apprentice Programs vs. College: What's the Cost?" *Blog.michiganconstruction.com*, 14 Nov. 2016, blog.michiganconstruction.com/apprentice-programs-vs-college-whats-the-cost-0.

Stahl, Ashley. "5 Industries Experiencing Double-Digit Growth over the next Decade." *Forbes*, 8 Apr. 2022, www.forbes.com/sites/ashleystahl/2022/04/08/5-industries-experiencing-double-digit-growth-over-the-next-decade/?sh=13a62dc613ec. Accessed 29 Apr. 2023.

"These Are the Most-Regretted College Majors." *NewsNation*, 14 Sept. 2022, www.newsnationnow.com/us-news/education/survey-these-are-the-top-college-majors-people-regret/#:~:text=(NewsNation)%20%E2%80%94%20Millions%20of%20college. Accessed 6 May 2023.

"Types of Apprenticeship | the Working Centre." *Www.theworkingcentre.org*, www.theworkingcentre.org/types-trades/931-types-apprenticeship. Accessed 23 Apr. 2023.

U.S. Department of Labor. "Data and Statistics | U.S. Department of Labor." *Www.dol.gov*, www.dol.gov/agencies/eta/apprenticeship/about/statistics/2021. Accessed 24 Apr. 2023.

Waters, Huw. "Thinking of a Career Change? Try an Apprenticeship." *Www.linkedin.com*, 31 Oct. 2016, www.linkedin.com/pulse/thinking-career-change-try-apprenticeship-huw-waters. Accessed 6 May 2023.

Welding, Lyss. "College Enrollment Statistics in the U.S. | BestColleges." *Www.bestcolleges.com*, 6 July 2022, www.bestcolleges.com/research/college-enrollment-statistics/. Accessed 24 Apr. 2023.

"Why a Mentally Challenging Job May Be Good for the Brain." *Fisher Center for Alzheimer's Research Foundation*, 10 Sept. 2021, www.alzinfo.org/articles/prevention/why-a-mentally-challenging-job-may-be-good-for-the-brain/#:~:text=The%20researchers%20found%20that%20those. Accessed 30 Apr. 2023.

Made in United States
Troutdale, OR
01/22/2024